DYNAMICS OF DALITS DEVELOPMENT

DYNAMICS OF DALITS DEVELOPMENT

E. D. SETTY, Ph.D.

AKANSHA PUBLISHING HOUSE
NEW DELHI-110002 (INDIA)

AKANSHA PUBLISHING HOUSE
4649-B/21, Ansari Road
Darya Ganj, New Delhi - 110 002
Email: ektabooks@yahoo.com
Ph. : 23263193 / 9811582579

Dynamics of Dalits Development

First Published 2007

ISBN : 978-81-8370-107-5

[The responsibility for the facts stated, conclusions reached etc. is entirely that of the Author. The publisher is not responsible for them, whatsoever.]

PRINTED IN INDIA

Published by **M.P. Misra for Akansha Publishing House**, New Delhi and Printed at Aryan Offset, Delhi.

Shri D.K. Adikesavulu
Member of Parliament
has sponsored and patronized
publication of this book

DEDICATED

TO

CHARANJIT SINGH ATWAL

Deputy Speaker, Lok Sabha

सत्यमेव जयते

BHAIRON SINGH SHEKHAWAT
VICE-PRESIDENT OF INDIA

Foreword

Poverty is a complex social problem encompassing a broad spectrum of issues. It affects 26 per cent of our population living below the poverty line who are deprived of basic amenities of life such as food, clothing, shelter, health, education and so on. The Supreme Court of India while recognising the debilitating impact of poverty on the quality of life, expanded the content and contour of the expression of 'life' in Article 21 of Indian Constitution and ruled that the right to life includes right to live with human dignity. It encompasses within its ambit the bare necessities of life which include not only health and sanitation, clothing and shelter but also protection and preservation of environment free from pollution of air and water. Thus, there is an obligation on the State to provide a decent standard of living to the indigent and downtrodden segments of our society.

Combined with this are several provisions in the Constitution, which provide for equality and prohibit specific kinds of discrimination such as those based on religion, race, caste, sex, place of birth or descent. The ideal of equality reflected in the Constitution is alive to the historical factors that contribute to social inequality and discrimination and obliges the State to adopt affirmative measures to eliminate inequalities and to provide opportunities for the meaningful exercise of fundamental rights. The principle underlying preferential treatment is that formal guarantees of equal rights are insufficient when past prejudices and resulting inequalities persist. To correct the imbalance as also to create enabling conditions by providing special care is a step forward towards ensuring equality. Enactment of special provisions to give preferential treatment for members of the Scheduled Tribes and Scheduled Castes, the Dalits, in the matter of public employment and seats in State-run educational institutions needs to be seen from the perspective of providing level playing field to the disadvantaged and deprived sections of our society. An all-round upgradation of their condition is the true test of our country's progressive march. Our Constitution enjoins upon us all to fulfill this sacred obligation in full measure to prove ourselves worthy of the great vision of the founding fathers of our Constitution.

No doubt, there has been some improvement in the conditions of Scheduled Castes and Scheduled Tribes. Several laws have been passed to prohibit discrimination and the practice of untouchability. Yet, this problem continues either overtly or covertly. A vast majority of our dalit population still live in rural areas where the discrimination is manifestly glaring. Dalit atrocities have also grown considerably, making a significant dent into our republican values of equality, justice and fraternity. This needs to be arrested forthwith and the confidence of our dalits on the system needs to be restored. Unless we ensure equality and non-discrimination, we cannot be able to build an inclusive society and ensure development of all sections of society.

Let us pledge to realise the dream of the Father of our Nation, Mahatma Gandhi to build an India in which **"there shall be no high class and low class of people . . . there can be no room in such an India for the curse of untouchability".** Development of dalits and overcoming their discrimination must get our undivided attention. Dr. B.R. Ambedkar in the course of the Constituent Assembly debates had warned that **"if inequality were not removed at the earliest possible moment those who suffer from inequality will blow up the structure of political democracy which this Assembly has so laboriously built**

up". Let us heed this warning carefully and take appropriate measures to strengthen the fabric of our society and the foundation of our democracy.

The author, Dr. E.D. Setty, has highlighted in this publication titled "Dynamics of Dalits Development" the issues causing poverty which are proving a hurdle in the empowerment of the dalits and multiple ways to tackle the problem. Based on his wide experience in dealing with rural development, one finds in this publication practical ideas and strategies which could be of great help to deal with poverty. As one could see in this publication, the emphasis is on clinical approach by including the people's participation and the involvement of the local leadership as the basis of realising the felt needs and aspirations of the people. This publication is indeed helpful to all those who are keen to bring about a sea change in the lives of the deprived sections of the society.

I congratulate Dr. Setty for highlighting the problems of the poor and the deprived and suggesting ways and means to ameliorate their condition. I am sure, this thought provoking book will be widely read and will be useful to the policy planners, administrators and all those committed to the welfare of this important segment of our society.

BHAIRON SINGH SHEKHAWAT

NEW DELHI
30th JANUARY, 2007
(Mahatma Gandhi's Martyrdom's Day)

Preface

Before we move into the Preface, I would like to briefly mention an anecdote which led to taking up the present study. I have proposed to Sri Chandrababu Naidu, Ex-Chief Minister of Andhra Pradesh, the following 4 book projects:

1. A Practical Guide on Working with People.
2. Clinical Approach to Alleviation of Poverty
3. Dynamics of Dalits Development
4. A Total Systems Approach to Village as a Unit of Development.

Sri Chandrababu Naidu has given me an appointment in February 2005. I went to his residence in Hyderabad on the date of appointment. I met him. Before we could discuss the above mentioned book projects there was a family waiting to meet him and he asked me to sit in a small room where usually he meets individuals on appointment. While he was with this family interacting in another larger room, I moved into as he asked me to a small room where he would meet me. In the small room when I entered I saw two people sitting on a bench. One I could recognise as a Minister in Sri Chandrababu Naidu's cabinet, but I was not able to recall his name. Next to me on my right side was another gentleman. I was sitting with these two people nearly for 10 minutes until the arrival of Sri Chandrababu Naidu. While I was sitting with these two people in the interview room, I kept silent and didn't have any interaction with my two neighbours. When Sri Chandrababu Naidu came and occupied his seat in front of us, I just tried to tell him that though the suffix in my name is Setty (E. Desingu Setty) for some clarity that I belong to Setty Balija community and that I am not a Vysya. On my sharing this real identity with Sri N. Chandrababu Naidu he immediately pointed out that the gentleman sitting on my right side on the bench is also Setty – Naidu a Balija. This man was Sri D.K. Adikesavulu – Member of Parliament. Though I have known his name for a couple of years, I have not seen him. Immediately I felt very happy that I was meeting Sri Adikesavulu and greeted him.

Then I briefly explained to Sri Chandrababu Naidu and Sri Adikesavulu the purpose and objectives that would be met with and their usefulness once the book projects are completed. In an unprecedented way Sri Adikesavulu with all the enthusiasm said that he would support two book projects mentioned below:

1. Clinical Approach to Alleviation of Poverty
2. Dynamics of Dalits Development.

In brief I would like to mention that Sri Adikesavulu is the patron of these two studies. The entire credit goes to him in bringing out these two books. Now we move on to the preface to this book.

We may briefly look into the contents of the chapters included in this book. The introductory part briefly discusses the origin and ramification of Varna and Caste System in India and the emergence of what was called Panchama and now designated as Dalits, constituents of the fourth Varna Sudra. Chapter 2 as the chapter heading indicates looks into the emergence of Varna and Caste System and how it proliferated in different forms during the later centuries as viewed by Indian and Western Scholars. We may take Chapter 2 as a brief critical review of the Institution of Varna – Caste system.

Chapter 3 is a detailed general picture of the Dalits in India numbering around 800 with different sub-castes with ethnic names. In order to study a sample of respondents belonging to the higher castes and also of Dalits – Mala and Madiga, Chapter 4 as a sample illustration brings out the functional relationships between the higher castes and the Dalits. Though it is a limited field study it is illustrative of the dynamics of relationship and attitudes on the part of both the higher castes and the Dalits. Chapter 5 brings out the feelings, opinions, attitudes, views and problems reflected in the case studies. Chapter 6 focuses on Influence of Caste on Development. Development cannot be mechanical. Social forces influence and operate on any development activity. Caste which is unique in the Indian context for several centuries, though it is on the decline still plays a significant role both as a positive and negative factor in the field of development of Dalits. The life of the scheduled castes has been a sad story for centuries. Though there are several provisions in helping and improving the life of Dalits, there is a need for special attention to be paid to them. Chapter 7 emphasises on integrated and comprehensive approach towards development of the Dalits encompassing political, economic, social, educational, psychological and cultural value system. It briefly spells out the aspects of development which have been established already and the kind of measures that are to be introduced and sustained related to other fields of development in respect to the Dalits. We may consider Chapter 8 as a basic and systematic process in formulating plans in meeting people's needs especially the downtrodden Dalits. It could definitely serve as a guide giving directions to the planners. They have to go about in formulating plans to meet people's needs. Chapter 9 speaks of the need to take each village as a unit of development. This operationally links to what is emphasised in Dalit Development. Chapter 10 speaks of the role of local institutions as primary agents of social change. In the entire gamut of Dalit and Rural Development, Local Leaders are expected to play a contributory role. Chapters 11 and 12 speak of the role of local leaders and youth in improving the conditions of the living in rural communities. Chapter 13 lays emphasis on the basic factor of healthy life – environmental sanitation as a significant factor contributing to health of people. Especially in the case of residences of Dalit communities, sanitation in majority of the cases is very poor. Chapter 14 suggests certain critical and highly relevant measures towards amelioration of the living conditions of the Dalits in India. The last chapter in summary form focuses on the perennial, sensitive, highly relevant and highly deserving and humanly justified measures to be adopted to see that the Dalits all over India live and lead life as respectable human individuals assured of minimum standard of life. The question of Dalits Development is a complex one, the attitudes, prejudices and the operative value system on the part of the higher caste and the Dalits are deep rooted, rather ingrained in the minds of people. One can hope with good intentions and with relevant ameliorative measures, a day will dawn in India that all the people in India irrespective of Varna, Caste, Religion and Sect are treated as individuals with equal status and recognition.

E. D. SETTY, Ph.D.

Acknowledgements

I would like to express my profoundest thanks to Sri Bhairon Singh Shekhawat, Vice-President of India for his highly valuable, significant and encouraging Foreword to this book.

I owe a great deal of thanks and indebtedness and heartfelt thanks to Sri D.K. Adikesavulu, Member of Parliament who has supported this book project. He is the patron of the study. Throughout the work of this book he has been the constant encouraging factor. I cannot simply say these things in words, but I owe him a great deal of indebtedness.

I am especially thankful to Sri P. Krishna Moorthy for his continued assistance and encouragement throughout the work of this book.

I would like to express my sincere thanks to the authors and publishers from which I have adopted some material for this book.

My sincere thanks to Sri S. Rama Krishna, Stenographer who has prepared the manuscript.

My sincere appreciation to my wife Smt. E. Vishalakshi, for her support and encouragement extended to me during the time I worked on this book.

E. D. SETTY, Ph.D.

Contents

CHAPTER 1

Introduction

Caste system is unique in India though we have three great races – Negroid, Mongoloid and Europoid and several sub-races. The boundaries among them have not been as severe as in respect to the hierarchy of caste system in India. Theoretically, traditionally it is described as based on division of labour. Though, it is justified in the name of division of labour over a period of 3 millennium the castes have become solidified with closed doors allowing and forbidding matrimonial alliances and inter-dining* with graded inequality. There are said to be around 3000 castes and sub-castes in India. In the present study we are focusing on Dalits numbering around 800 sub-castes and they go by different names in the regional languages. Mainly the Mala, the Madiga or the Chamars in South India are well-known ethnic groups within Dalits. The nomenclature Dalit is a recent one and it is a generic term used for all groups under earlier so-called untouchable groups (Chapter 3 in the book deals with a brief anthropological description of Dalits in India).

It is most unfortunate that the Dalits over centuries were treated so badly even lower than the animals. Though India claims and feels proud of its great traditions and its contribution to civilization and literature and especially to religion and philosophy, its record in respect to the Dalits is a stigma. It reflects the way the innumerable so called higher castes have treated the Dalits in every aspect of human

* Chapter 2 provides a brief account of caste system in India.

interaction and human dignity. The higher castes maintain distance.

For centuries together the Dalits in a mute way accepted and endured the isolation and social restrictions imposed on them.

The advocates of caste system justified the stratification and graded inequality saying the *Varna* System was created by God and one's birth is attributed to his *karma* in his previous birth. This is a stand they have taken and the justification they advocated over the pitiable and deplorable conditions of life in respect of the Dalits in India. One should be ashamed of this. Even the educated have treated the Dalits as sub-human and menial.

With the abolition of untouchability and reservation for the Dalits in respect to admission to educational institutions and jobs in Government Departments and extension of economic benefits in terms of land allocation, housing, financial assistance for petty business, the scenario in respect to Dalits all over the country is changing. Another significant impetus for elevating theoretically the image and the importance accorded to them is periodic elections to the State Assemblies and the Parliament. Even though, they were treated for centuries as menial and lowly, the politicians seek their votes in their favour. The adult suffrage which is the right for every adult citizen of India has boosted the importance of Dalits in India who constitute around 17 percent of the total population.

We could see gradually changing behaviour on the part of the Dalits and the so called higher castes, but as it is quiet known in the villages though the distance between the higher castes and Dalits is rather reduced still the distance is maintained. One can write volumes on the dynamics of caste system and its long history. By virtue of reservations for admission to educational programmes, State and Union services, the Dalits enjoy certain percentage of admissions and jobs, but regretfully and unfortunately those who have been fortunate to hold higher administrative and ministerial jobs exclude themselves and distance themselves in many cases from their Dalit communities. It is reported that these

Dalit babus promote their own children and relatives and grow into a rich and well recognised affluent sub-groups within the Dalit community. The law does not interfere here. Unfortunately, there are divisive forces in ethnic sense among the Dalits. The Mala and Madiga are the North and South Pole. You may bring in change in interaction and acceptance, closeness between the Brahmin and other castes and the so called low caste Dalits. But to bring together the Mala and Madiga as it has been, as it appears today is impossible. Though they fight for some privileges, better treatment and incentives financial and material for their onward progress, the Mala and Madiga distance themselves socially and psychologically though they may be close to each other residentially. It is really amazing and difficult to understand though the Mala and Madiga especially in South India come under the generic term Dalits and they don't see eye to eye, absolutely no marital relations and inter dining. Today, they are fighting in A.P. through their organisations demanding classification of Dalits into sub-categories, sub-ethnic groups within the Mala and Madiga communities.

The younger generation among the Dalits some of them with primary and collegiate education and with increased awareness as to what is entitled to them, have become a movement in several parts of the country demanding justice in terms of constitution and legislative measures which focuses on educational and job opportunities. During the past couple of decades the Dalits all over India have become alert and thought that they have to make use of the provisions and the struggling to avail themselves of these opportunities offered for their growth and development. Gradually they have to wriggle out of age long mire where they suffered as sub-human beings. But when it comes to availing the opportunities offered both by the centre and state administration, it is left to the initiative on the part of the Dalits availing of these opportunities. At this point of time, measures are initiated and inducted into the system of administration and law for specific efforts to be made and privileges provided, in the name of justice and in the egalitarian sense to the Dalit communities.

CHAPTER 2

Emergene of Varna and Caste System in India: A Brief Critical Review

The emergence *Varna* and Caste system is attributed to a divine order that it was the God who has created the *Chatur Varnas* based on the *Guna-Vibhaga* and *Karma-Vibhaga*. Here we may quote the *sloka* from the *Bhagavadgita*.

Chaatur-Varnam Mayaa Srishtam Guna-Karma Vibhaagabah.
Tasya Kartaara Mapi Maam Viddhya-Kartaara Kavyayam.

(Chapter 4, *Sloka* 13)

Since the *Varna* – caste system is unique in India, we come across different views as believed and envisaged by Indian thinkers and people from western countries. We reproduce in the following pages views of some western thinkers and writers from sources noted below.

It may look to the reader redundant and repetitive but some of the ideas and explanations in respect to *Varna* and Caste system are worth to be noted.

When we speak of Dalits—the new name being used recently for the Harijans, there is a need to go into some reflections on the origin of what is called caste system. In the following pages we will look into some of the controversies in respect of the emergence of four Varnas—Brahmana, Kshatriya, Vysya and Sudra.

Caste - The term Caste, derived from the Portuguese *Casta*, expressive of the Indian word Jati, has been universally adopted by Europeans to denote the different classes or tribes into which the people of India are divided. "The permanent division of the community into classes, with hereditary professions assigned to each, is one of the most remarkable institutions of Hindustan. There are four great divisions. The most distinguished of all is that of Brahmana or Brahmans, who are said to have come from the mouth of Brahma: the second in rank is that of Kshatriya or Rajas, from the arm of Brahma: the third the Vysya or merchants from the thigh of Brahma, the fourth, the Sudras or workmen, from his foot: all with their females. Each of these four tribes is subdivided into several more; the Sudras especially have an almost endless number of distinctions; such as herdsmen who keep the cows; shepherds who tend the sheep; weavers; five castes of Artisans, viz., carpenters, goldsmiths, blacksmiths, stone-cutters, and founders. The several castes of cultivators take precedence of other Sudras, and look with contempt on tradesmen and labourers. There is a Caste of Kallaru, or robbers, who consider their profession as no way discreditable to themselves or their tribe. Each caste exhibits some particular and local varieties of its own by which it is discriminated from the rest: Some distinguish themselves by the cut and colour of their clothes; some by the manner in which they put them on. But however extravagant their modes and customs are, they never excite from castes of the most opposite habits and fashions the least appearance of contempt or dislike. Upon this point there seems to be the most perfect toleration.

In the south of India there is another division of the different tribes still more general than those which have been yet mentioned. It is that of Right-hand and Left-hand Castes. The greater number of Hindu castes belongs either to the Right-hand or the Left. The Brahmana, the Pariahs (or outcastes) and several tribes of the Sudras, are considered neutral, and enjoying all the privileges and honours attached to both hands, they take no part with either. These neutral castes are frequently called upon to arbitrate in the fierce disputes that occur between the Right and Left-hand parties. Both parties lay claim to certain privileges; and when any encroachment is made by either it is followed by tumults that spread through a district, accompanied with every excess; and generally with bloody contests; The Hindu, usually so gentle and timid, seems to change his nature. There is no danger he fears to encounter in maintaining these rights.

Dr. Muir in the first volume of his O.S. Texts, has very fully investigated the mythical accounts of the creation of man and of the origin of the four castes. He says "it will be seen from the texts adduced that from a very early period the Indian writers, origin of mankind and of the classes or castes into which they found their own community divided. The most commonly received of these explanations is the fable which represents the Brahmans, Kshatriyas, Vysyas and sudras, to have been separately created from the head, the breast or arms, the thighs, and the feet of the Creator. Of this mythical account no trace is to be found to any of the hymns of the Rig Veda, except one, the Parusha Sukta."

Dr. Muir is of opinion that this hymn belongs to the most recent portion of the Rig Veda. Mr. Colebrook, Professors Max Muller and Weber concur on this view; which however is controverted by Dr. Haug.

After quoting a great number of texts from the oldest authorities, Dr. Muir remarks: "When we discover in the most ancient Indian writings such different and even discrepant accounts of the origin of man, all put forth with equal positiveness, it is impossible to imagine that any uniform explanation of the diversity of castes could have been received at the period when they were composed, or to regard any of the texts which have been cited as more orthodox and authoritative than the rest. Even, therefore, if we should suppose that the author of the *Purusha Sukta* meant to represent the four castes as having literally sprung from separate parts of Purusha's body, it is evident that the same idea was not always or even generally adopted by those who followed him, as a revealed truth in which they were bound to acquiesce. In fact, nothing is clearer than that in all these cosmogonies, the writers, of their descriptions, gave the freest scope to their individual fancy in the invention of details. In such circumstances, perfect coincidence cannot be expected in the narratives."

The following are the results of Dr. Muir's careful investigation of all the Texts bearing on the subject:

"The details which I have supplied in the course of this chapter must have rendered it abundantly evident that the sacred books of the Hindus contain no uniform or consistent account of the origin of castes; but, on the contrary, present the greatest varieties of speculation on this subject. Explanations mystical, mythical, and rationalistic, are all offered in turn; and the freest scope is given by the individual writers to fanciful and arbitrary conjecture.

First: We have the set of accounts in which the four castes are said to have sprung from progenitors who were separately created; but in regard to the manner of their creation we find the greatest diversity of statement. The most common story is that the castes issued from the mouth, arms, thighs and feet of Purusha, or Brahma. The oldest extant passage in which this idea occurs and from which all the later myths of a similar tenor have no doubt been borrowed, is, as we have seen, to be found in the *Purusha Sukta*; but it is doubtful whether, in the form in which it is there presented, this representation is anything more than an allegory. In some of the texts which I have quoted from the *Bhagavata Purana*, traces of the same allegorical character may be perceived; but in Manu and the Puranas the mystical import of the Vedic text disappears and the figurative narrative is hardened into a literal statement of fact. In other passages, where a separate origin is assigned to the castes, they are variously said to have sprung from the word *Bhuh*, *Bhuvah*, *Svah*; from different Vedas; from different sets of prayers; from the gods and the asuras; from nonentity and from the imperishable, the perishable and other principles. In the chapters of the *Vishnu*, *Vayu* and *Markandeya Puranas*, where castes are described as coeval with the creation and as having been naturally distinguished by different gunas, or qualities, involving varieties of moral character, we are nevertheless allowed to infer that those qualities exerted no influence on the classes in whom they were inherent, as the condition of the whole race during the Krita age is described as one of uniform perfection and happiness; while the actual separation into castes did not take place, according to the *Vayu Purana*, until men become deteriorated in the Treta age.

Second: In various passages from the Brahmanas, Epic poems and Puranas, the creation of mankind is, as we have seen, described without the least allusion to any separate production of the progenitors of the four castes. And whilst in the chapters where they relate the distinct formation of the castes, the Puranas, as has been observed, assign different natural dispositions to each class, they elsewhere represent all mankind as being at the creation uniformly distinguished by the quality of passion. In one of the texts I have quoted, men are said to be the offspring of Vivasvat; in another his son Manu is said to be their progenitor; whilst in a third they are said to descended from a female of the same name. The passage which declares Manu to have been the father of the human race explicitly affirms that men of all the four castes were descended from him. In another remarkable text the *Mahabharata* categorically asserts that originally there was no distinction of classes, the existing distribution having arisen out of differences of character and occupation. Similarly, the *Bhagavata Purana* in one place informs us that in the Krita age there was but one caste; and this view appears also to be taken in some passages which I have adduced from the Epic poems.

In these circumstances, we may fairly conclude that the separate origination of the four castes was far from being an article of belief universally received by Indian antiquity.

Further, we may look into another source with more details on *Varna* - Caste System.

When the Aryans entered India there was already a class division in their tribal structure. Even in the earliest hymns we read of the Ksatra, the nobility and the vis, the ordinary tribesmen and the records of several other early Indo-European peoples suggest that a tribal aristocracy was a feature of Indo-European society even before the tribes migrated from their original home. As they settled among the darker aboriginals the Aryans seem to have laid greater stress than before on purity of blood and class divisions hardened, to exclude those Dasa who had found a place on the fringes of Aryan and adopted their ways. Both these groups sank in the social scale. At the same time the priests, whose sacrificial lore was becoming more and more complicated and who therefore required greater skill and training, were arrogating higher privileges to themselves. By the end of the Rig Vedic period society was divided into four great classes and this fourfold division was given religious sanction and looked on as fundamental. This is evident from one of the most important hymns of the collection, in which the four classes are said to have emanated from the dismembered primeval man, who was sacrificed by the gods at the beginning of the world.

[Source: Adopted from the Book "*A Classical Dictionary of India*" by John Garrett, Delhi-110052.]

The four classes, the priest (brahmana), warrior (Ksatriya), peasant (Vysya) and serf (Sudra), were crystallizing throughout the period of the *Rig Veda*. They have survived to the present day. The Sanskrit word used for them, varna, means "colour", and itself indicates their origin in the development complexion and alien culture. The term varna does not mean "caste" and has never meant "caste", by which convenient word it is often loosely translated.

The basic unit of Aryan Society was the family. A group of related families formed a sept or grama, a term which later regularly meant "village", but which in the Rig Veda usually refers to a group of kinsfolk rather than to a settlement. The family was staunchly patrilinear and patriarchal. The wife, though she enjoyed a respectable position, was definitely subordinate to her husband. Marriage was usually monogamous and apparently indissoluble, for no reference to divorce or the remarriage of widow occurs in the Rig Veda.

LAWS OF CLASS AND STAGE OF LIFE

Often and in many contexts we read of "the Dharma of class and stage of life" (*varnasrama-dharma*), which, in the golden age of the remote past, was self-evident and uninfringed, but which is now vague, misunderstood and partly forgotten, and which the brahmans interpret and the king preserves and enforces. The implication of this phrase is that Dharma is not the same for all. There is indeed common Dharma, a general norm of conduct which all must follow equally, but there is also a dharma appropriate to each class and to each stage in the life of the individual. The dharma of men of high birth is not that of humbler folk and the dharma of the student is not that of the old man.

This thorough going recognition that men are not the same and that there is a hierarchy of classes, each with its separate duties and distinctive way of life, is one of the most striking features of ancient Indian sociology. Criticisms of the pretensions of the higher classes were heard from time to time and equalitarian propositions were occasionally put forward, but in general this concept has held its ground from the end of the Rigvedic period to the present day.

THE FOUR GREAT CLASSES

By the end of the Rigvedic period the fourfold division of society was regarded as fundamental, primeval and divinely ordained. The four Varnas of India developed out of very early Aryan class divisions, for some class stratification existed in many Indo-European communities and ancient Iran had four pistras or classes, comparable in some respects to those of India. In India class stratification grew more rigid when, in the Vedic period, a situation arose rather like that prevailing in South Africa today, with a dominant fair minority striving to maintain its purity and its supremacy over a darker majority. Tribal class-divisions hardened and the dark-skinned aboriginal found a place only in the basement of the Aryan social structure, as a serf with few rights and many disabilities. Soon the idea of varna had become so deeply embedded in the Indian mind that its terminology was even used for the classification of precious commodities such as pearls and useful materials like timber. Theoretically all Aryans belonged to one of the four classes, with the exception of children, ascetics and widows, who were outside the system.

Varna came to the Dravidian South comparatively late, for the earliest Tamil literature shows a society divided into tribal groups with little sense of the precedence of one over the other. Succeeding centuries saw the gradual hardening of class, until South Indian brahmans became even stricter in their ritual observances and the untouchables even more debased than in the North.

A sharp distinction was made between the three higher classes and the sudra. The former were twice-born (*dvija*), once at their natural birth and again at their initiation, when they were invested with the sacred thread and received into Aryan society.* The sudra had no initiation and was often not looked on as Aryan at all. The fourfold division was in theory functional. Manu lays down that the duty of the Brahman is to study and teach, to sacrifice and to give and receive gifts; the Kshatriya must protect the people, sacrifice and study; the Vysya also sacrifices and studies, but his chief function is to breed cattle, to till the earth, to pursue trade and to lend money; the Sudra's duty is only to serve the three higher classes – and" it is better", Manu adds elsewhere, "to do one's own duty badly than another's well". This epigram, elaborated so beautifully in the *Bhagavad-Gita*. Gita, was the leading theme of most Indian social thought; for each man there was a place in society and a function to fulfil, with its own duties and rights.

This was the ideal, but though in the Middle Ages it was perhaps approached, it has never been wholly reached. The precepts of the texts which lay down the laws for the conduct of the four classes were rarely fully carried out in practice and were often blatantly infringed. The texts were written by brahmans and from the brahmanic point of view and represent conditions as the brahmans would have liked them to be. Thus it is not surprising that they claim the utmost honour for the priestly class and exalt it above measure.

The Brahman was a great divinity in human form. His spiritual power was such that he could instantly destroy the king and his army, if they attempted to infringe his rights. In law he claimed great privileges and in every respect he demanded precedence, honour and worship. Even the Buddhist

---

* In later texts the term "twice-born" was often reserved for Brahmans, but strictly it applies to Kshatriyas and Vaisyas also if they have been initiated.

scriptures, though they do not admit the more extravagant brahmanical claims and regularly exalt the kshatriya over the Brahman, recognize his greatness, if he is pious and sincere.

These Buddhist sources show us two types of Brahman. There were learned brahmans, performing all the rites of the Aryan and receiving great respect; but there were also village brahmans, who made much of their living by fortune-telling and sorcery and who were less honoured. For all the rigidity of the class system the brahmans soon lost their racial purity and it has even been suggested that, as Aryan culture expanded, schools of aboriginal sorcerers and medicine men managed to obtain a footing in the brahmanic order, just as aboriginal chiefs were certainly assimilated to the warrior class. Thus, it may well be the proto-Hinduism of the Harappa culture was ultimately assimilated to the Aryan faith.

Of professional priests there were various types and classes – in the earliest times we read of the semi-legendary *Rishis*, or seers, who composed the Vedic hymns, while the sacrificial ritual demanded a number of priests *(ritivi)* with specialized duties – invokers (hotri), cantor's mony (adhvaryu). The term brahmana meant originally "one possessed of Brahman", a mysterious magical force of the type widely known to modern anthropologists by the Polynesian word *mana*. It was first applied to the specially trained priest who superintendent the whole sacrifice and was ready to counterpart with his magic spells any evil influence caused by minor errors of ritual. By the end of the Rigvedic period the term used for all members of the priestly class.

There were other divisions within the order. The brahmans of the later Vedic period were divided into exogamous septs (gotra), a system which was copied in part by other classes and has survived to the present day. Later the Brahman class formed many castes, linked together by endogamy and common practices. A further division was the sakha or branch, based on the recension of the Vedic texts accepted as authoritative by the family in question.

Often the Brahman lived under the patronage of a king or chief and was provided for by grants of tax-free land, farmed by peasants, who would pay their taxes to the Brahman instead of to the king; but there were also land-owning brahmans who cultivated large estates by hired labour or sears might have a high post at court, and the purohita's* importance in the state has already been noted. Other brahmans might earn a competence as teachers of the Veda and the other branches of learning.

At all times many brahmans led truly religious lives. Kalidasa's Sakuntala gives a charming picture of a settlement of such pious brahmans, living simply but not too austerely in huts in the forest, woodland was forever perfumed with the fragrance of their sacred fires. Such Brahman colonies were supported by the gifts of kings and chiefs and of the peasants of the neighbourhood. Other brahmans became solitary ascetics, while in the middle Ages brahmany monastic orders were founded, rather on the Buddhist model.

But the varied religious activity of ancient India did not provide a livelihood for more than a few of the brahmans. The Smriti literature contains special sections "on duty when in distress" (apad-dharma), which carefully define what a man may legitimately do when he cannot earn a living by the profession normally followed by his class and by these provisions brahmans might pursue all manner of trades and professions. Many were employed in important government posts and several royal families were of Brahman origin. Generally the law books disapprove of brahmans engaging in agriculture, because it inflicts injury on animals and insects, but this rule was often ignored. A Brahman is forbidden to trade in certain commodities – among them cattle and other animals, slaves, weapons and spirituous liquor – and his lending money at interest is also disapproved of, though Manu allows him to lend at low interest to "wicked people", by whom he probably means those who do not maintain Aryan rites. But though he kept these rules rigidly, a Brahman would find trades and professions open to him.

---

* This term was extended to mean a priest, who performed the many rites and ceremonies of Hinduism for a family or group of families and has survived in this sense to the present day.

Opinions differed as to whether a Brahman engaged in a secular profession was worthy of the respect accorded to the practicing member of his class and no clear ruling is laid down. As far as can be gathered from general literature the special rights of the Brahman were usually only granted to those who lived by sacrifice and teaching. Carudatta, the poor Brahman hero of the play, "The Little Clay Cart" receives scurvy treatment at the hands of the court, probably because he is a Brahman by birth only and not by profession.

For all his prestige, the Brahman was often the butt of satire. Even in the Rigveda the croaking of frogs at the beginning of the rainy season is compared to the monotonous reciting of the priests, though here no sarcasm may be intended. But there can be no other explanation of a remarkable passage in the early Chandogya Upanishad, which describes a vision of the sage Vaka Dalbhya, wherein dogs move round in a circle, each holding the tail of the preceding dog in its mouth, "just as the priests do when about to sing praises"; and then, repeating the very sacred syllable Om, they sing: "Om! Let us eat! Om! Let us drink! Om! May the gods Varuna, Prajapati and brahmans occurs in the Aitaraya Brahmana, in an interesting passage which describes the other three classes from the point of view of the warrior; here the Brahman is "a receiver of gifts, a drinker of soma, an eater of food, to be expelled at will". The vidusaka, the fool of Sanskrit drama, an amiable but gluttons figure of fun, is invariably a brahman.

There are, however, few frontal attacks on brahmanical pretensions, even in the literature of the Buddhists, who came nearest to an anti-brahmanical point of view; but one brief Buddhist tract, the "Diamond Needle" (Vajrasuci), ascribed to Asvaghosa, of the 1st or 2nd century A.D., attacks the claims of the priesthood and indirectly the whole class system, with vigorous dialectical skill. The claims of the Brahman were, in fact, often ignored and not wholly unchallenged.

The second class was the ruling one, the members of which were in the Vedic period called rajanya and later kshatriya. The theoretical duty of the Kshatriyas was "protection", which included fighting in war and governing in peace. In early times he often claimed precedence over the Brahman; this claim is implicit in the *Aitareya Brahmana* passage which we have quoted, the inclusion of which in a brahmanical scripture is hard to account for. According to Buddhist tradition, in times when the brahmans are the highest class Buddhas are born in that class, while when Kshatriyas are the highest they are born as Kshatriyas. The historical Buddha was a Kshatriya and his followers evidently had few doubts about class priorities. Where the names of the four classes are mentioned together in the Pali scriptures that of the Kshatriyas usually comes first.

A strong king was always a check on brahmanic pretensions, just as the brahmans were a check on the pretensions of the king. Tradition speaks of many anti-brahmanical kings who came to evil ends and the legend of Parusurama, who destroyed the whole ksatriya class for its impiety, must contain a recollection of fierce strife between the two classes in pre-Buddhist times. After the Mauryan period the brahman's theoretical position was established throughout most of India, but the Kshatriya was in fact still often his equal or superior.

The martial class of ancient India, from great emperors to petty chiefs, was recruited from all races and ranks and all the invaders of India down to the coming of the Muslims were given a place in the social order in this way. Manu describes the warlike peoples on the fringes of Aryan civilization, including the Greeks (*Yavana*), the Scythes (*Saka*) and the Parthians (*Pahlava*), as Kshatriyas who had fallen from grace through their neglect of the Sacred Law, but who could be received once more into the Aryan fold by adopting the orthodox way of life and performing appropriate penitential sacrifices. This provision might be applied to almost any conquering people and the Rajputs, in later times the Kshatriyas *par excellence*, were no doubt largely descended from such invaders.

The Kshatriyas claimed and received certain privileges. They continued old customs not in keeping with orthodoxy, with such persistence that the brahmanic law givers were forced to give them legal status. Thus marriage by capture was permitted to the Kshatriya, as were the clandestine liaison with svayamvara, at which a girl chose her husband from among the assembled suitors. Like the brahmans, they did not always live by fulfilling their ideal function. The rules of *apad-dharma* applied to them also and there are many records of men of warrior becoming merchants and craftsmen.

In Vedic times the Vysya, or mercantile class, though entitled to the services passage of the priesthood and to the sacred thread of initiation, was but a poor third to the brahmans and Kshatriyas. In the *Aitareya Brahmana* passage the vysya is described as "paying tribute to another, to be lived on by another, to be oppressed at will". Other passages in early brahmanic literature show him as a wrenched and down-trodden cultivator or petty merchant, who is of no interest to his betters except as a source of profit.

According to Manu the special duty of the vysya was keeping cattle, which were made over to his charge at the creation of the world. The class evidently originated in the ordinary peasant tribesmen of the *Rigveda*, but long before the law book ascribed to Manu was composed, it had many activities. The sudras, the humblest of the four classes, had by now taken to agriculture. The ideal vysya has expert knowledge of jewels, metals, cloth, threads, spices and all manner of merchandise – he is, in fact, the ancient Indian business-man.

Though the Brahmana literature gives the vysya few rights and humble status, the Buddhist and Jaina scriptures, a few centuries later in date and of more easterly provenance, show that he was not always oppressed in practice. They mention many wealthy merchants living in great luxury and powerfully organized in guilds. Here the ideal vysya is not the humble tax paying cattle-breeder, but the *asitikotivibhava*, the man possessing eight million panas. Wealthy vysyas were respected by kings and enjoyed their favour and confidence. It was they, rather than the Kshatriyas, who chiefly favoured the rising unorthodox religions of Buddhism and Jainism. They formed by this time, at least in the regions of Magadha and Kosala, a true bourgeoisie, no doubt small in number, but very important. Numerous inscriptions from Sunga times onwards record the great donations of vysya merchants and skilled craftsmen to religious causes, especially to Buddhism and show that they were prosperous and influential.

If the vysya, according to the *Aitareya Brahmana*, was to be oppressed at will, the lot of the *sudra* was even more unfortunate. He was "the servant of another, to be expelled at will, to be slain at will" –but the latter phrase may be interpreted" to be beaten at will" and the import of the whole passage seems to be satirical.

Sudras were not "twice-born". For them there was no initiation into full Aryan status and they were not regularly considered Aryans, though the *Arthasastra* in its chapters on slavery specifically mentions them as such. The sudra was in fact a second-class citizen, on the fringes of Aryan society. The word sudra is of doubtful etymology and occurs only once in the Rig Veda; it was perhaps originally the name of a non-Aryan tribe, which became subordinate to the conquerors and the origin of the sudra class may be accounted for in this way, though it certainly included other elements. As the rigidity of brahmanic observances increased, groups which refused to accept orthodox custom, or clung to old practices which were no longer respectable, fell to the rank of sudras. There are today castes which themselves claim to be Kshatriyas, but which are branded by the brahmans as sudras because they adhere to customs which have long become objectionable, such as meat eating or the remarriage of widows. Persons born illegitimately, even when of pure high-class blood, were officially counted as sudras.

Sudras were of two kinds, "pure" or "not-excluded" (aniravasita) and "excluded" (niravasita). The latter were quite outside the pale of Hindu society and were virtually indistinguishable from the great body of people later known as untouchables. The distinction was made on the basis of the customs of the Sudra group in question and the profession followed by its members. According to the brahmanical textbooks the chief duty of the pure sudra was to wait on the other three classes. He was to eat the remnants of his master's food, wear his cast-off clothing and use his old furniture. Even when he had the opportunity of becoming wealthy he might not do so, "for a sudra who makes money is distressing to the brahmans". He had few rights and little value was set on his life in law. A Brahman killing a sudra performed the same penance as for killing a cat or dog. The sudra was not allowed to hear or repeat the Vedas. A land where sudras were numerous would suffer great misery.

Thus the textbooks give small hope of happiness to the wretched sudra, who could do little but serve his betters in unpleasant and servile tasks and whose only hope was rebirth in a higher social class; but there is good evidence that sudras did not always live the humble and wretched life laid down for them in the Sacred Law. There is mention of sudras engaged in manufacture and commerce and by Mauryan times many sudras were free peasants. The sudra had a place of sorts in the Hindu fold and was encouraged to imitate the customs of the higher classes. Though he might not hear the Vedas, the Epics and Puranas were open to him and he had a part in the devotional religion which became more and more popular from post-Mauryan times onwards and ultimately eclipsed the older cults; in the *Bhagwad Gita* Lord Krishna himself promises full salvation to those sudras who turn to him. From the point of view of most medieval sects, class and caste were affairs of the body rather than of the spirit and verses expressing the fundamental equality of all men are to be found in Dravidian devotional literature and in vernacular religious literature of later times. Theoretically Buddhism and Jainism made no class distinction in religious affairs. As we have seen, sudra kings were not known and many sudras, despite the injunctions of the law books, must have been prosperous.

UNTOUCHABLES

Below the sudras were the early representatives of the people who were later called untouchables, outcastes, depressed classes, or scheduled castes. Buddhist literature and the early Dharma Sutras show that several centuries before Christ there already existed groups of people who, though serving the Aryans in very menial and dirty tasks, were looked on as quite outside the pale. Sometimes they were called the "fifth class" (panchama), but most authorities rejected this term, as if to insist that they were excluded from the Aryan social order altogether.

Numerous groups of these people are mentioned, by names which are non-Aryan in origin and were probably those of aboriginal tribes which came under the sway of the advancing Aryans. Chief of these groups was the Candala, a term which came too used loosely for many types of untouchable. The Candala was not allowed to live in an Aryan town or village, but had to dwell in special quarters outside the boundaries. Though some Candalas had other means of livelihood, in theory their main task was the carrying and cremation of corpses and they also served as executioners of criminals.

According to the law books the Candala should be dressed in the garments of the corpses he cremated, should eat his food from broken vessels and should wear only iron ornaments. No man of higher class might have any but the most distant a relations with a Candala, on pain of losing his religious purity and falling to the candala's level. By Gupta times Candalas had become so strictly untouchable that, like lepers in medieval Europe, they were forced to strike a wooden clapper on entering a town, to warn the Aryans of their polluting approach.

Certain classes of outcastes or untouchables seem to have gained their unenviable position through the growth of the sentiment of non-violence – for instance the Nisala, who was a hunter, the fishing caste called Kaivarta and the leather worker (*Karavara*). The *pukkusa,* who appears as a sweeper in Buddhist literature, may have fallen in status because members of his class made and sold alcoholic liquor. More difficult to account for are such base classes as basket-maker (vena) and the chariot-maker (*rathakara*). In early Vedic times the latter was a most respected craftsmen, but soon fell to the status of an impure Sudra or outcaste.

By beginning of the Christian era the outcastes themselves had developed a caste hierarchy and had their own outcastes. Manu mentions the *antyavasayin*, a cross between a Candala and a nisada, who was despised even by the Candalas themselves. In later India every untouchable group imagined that some other group was lower than itself and this stratification evidently began quite early.

Even the lowest of the untouchable was not altogether without hope. Though he was denied access to the temples and the comforts of orthodox religion, Buddhist monks preached to him and the more enlightened wandering ascetics would give him instruction. The untouchable dying in defence of brahmans, cows, women and children secured a place in heaven. Orthodox texts contain frequent warnings on the evils which arise when Sudras and outcastes grow too powerful and this would seem to show that a candela might occasionally become influential.

Another class of untouchable was the *mleccha*, the word commonly used for outer barbarians of whatever race or colour. As an invader he was loathed, but once he had come into contact with Indian ways and was less strange and forbidding his status might improve. In fact it was not blood which made a group untouchable, but conduct. Generally there was no chance of an individual rising in the social scale, but for a group this was possible, over a number of generations, by adopting more orthodox practices and following the rules of the Smritis. Thus the Indian class system was always somewhat fluid.

CASTE

Relations between classes and social groups in later Hinduism were governed by rules of endogamy (marriage was only legitimate within the group), commensality (food was only to be received from and eaten in the presence of members of the same or a higher group) and craft-exclusiveness (each man was to live by the trade or profession of his own group and not take up that of another). Megasthenes noted seven endogamous and craft-exclusive classes in India – philosophers, peasants, herdsmen, craftsmen and traders, soldiers, government officials and councillors. His sevenfold division is certainly false, but he gives evidence to show that in Mauryan times class divisions were already hardening. Even in the Gupta period, however, the regulations were by no means rigid. Hypergamous inter-marriage was recognised, the rule of craft-exclusiveness was often ignored, or circumvented by the convenient escape clauses of *apad-dharma* and in the earlier law books the Brahman was permitted to accept food from any Aryan. It was only in late medieval times that it was finally recognised that exogamy and sharing meals with members of other classes were quite impossible for respectable people. These customs and many others such as widow-remarriage, were classed as *kalivarjya* – customs once permissible, but to be avoided in this dark Kali age, when men are no longer naturally righteous.

When the Portuguese came to India in the 16th century they found the Hindu community divided into many separate groups, which they called castes, meaning tribes, clans or families. The name stuck and became the usual word for the Hindu social group. In attempting to account for the remarkable proliferation of castes in 18th and 19th century India, authorities credulously accepted the traditional view that by a process of intermarriage and subdivision the 3,000 or more castes of modern India had evolved from the four primitive classes and the term "caste" were applied indiscriminately to both *varna* or class and *jati* or caste proper. This is a false terminology; castes formed, but the four great classes are stable. They are never more or less than four and for over 2,000 years their order of precedence has not altered. All ancient Indian sources make a sharp distinction between the two terms; *varna* is much referred to, but *jati* very little, comparatively rigid and exclusive social groups of later times. If caste is defined as a system of groups within the class, which are normally endogamous, commensal and craft-exclusive, we have no real evidence of its existence until comparatively late times.

Caste is the development of thousands of years, from the association of many different racial and other groups in a single cultural system. It is impossible to show its origin conclusively and we can do little more than faintly trace its development, since early literature paid scant attention to it; but it is practically certain that caste did not originate from the four classes. Admittedly it developed later than they, but this proves nothing. There are subdivisions in the four classes at a very early date, but the Brahman *gothras*, which go back to Vedic times, are not castes, since the gothras are exogamous and members of the same gothra are to be found in many castes.

Perhaps the first faint trace of caste is to be found in the careful cataloguing of trades and professions in later Vedic literature, as if their members were looked on almost as distinct species. In the Pali scriptures many trades and professions are described as living robbers and of separate quarters in the towns for different trades and professions. Many trades were organized in guilds, in which some authorities have seen the origin of the trade castes; but these trade groups cannot be counted as fully developed castes. A 5th century inscription form Mandasor shows us a guild of silk-weavers emigrating in a body from Lata (the region of the lower Narmada) to Mandasor and taking up many other crafts and professions, from soldering to astrology, but still maintaining its guild-consciousness. We have no evidence that this group was endogamous or commensal, and it was certainly not craft-exclusive; but its strong corporate sense was well aware of the four classes and also mentioned many mixed classes, no doubt accepting the orthodox view of the time that these sprang from the intermarriage of the four, but he shows no clear knowledge of the existence of caste in its modern form.

To present day the life of the lower orders is much more affected by caste than by varna – it is not being a vysya or a sudra, but being an *Ahir*, a *Kayasath*, or a *Sonar* which matters and corporate feeling is centred around this caste group, whether based on region, race, profession or religion. The same strong corporate sense existed at an even earlier date can be gathered from many sources. Indian society developed a very complex social structure, arising partly from tribal affiliations and partly from professional associations, which was continuously being elaborated by the introduction of new racial groups into the community and by the development of new crafts. In the Middle Ages the system became more or less rigid and the social group was now a caste in the modern sense. Professor J.H. Hutton has interpreted the caste system as an adaptation of one of the most primitive of social relationships, whereby a small clan, living in a comparatively isolated village, would hold itself aloof from its neighbours by a complex system of taboos and he has found embryonic caste features in the social structure of some of the wild tribes of present-day India. The caste system may well be the natural response of the many small and primitive peoples who were forced to come to terms with a more complex economic and social system. It did not develop out of the four Aryan Varnas and the two systems have never been thoroughly harmonized.

By the end of our period many of the present-day caste groups were already in existence. Even the Brahman class was much subdivided into endogamous groups, often based on locality and race, with many different practices. The Rajputs were divided into clans which, if not regularly endogamous, were castes of a sort and the Vysyas, Sudras and untouchables had evolved hundreds of castes. They were governed by local committees of elders, usually hereditary, which had the power to expel members and regulate caste rules and whose decisions, from the time of the *Arthasastra* onwards, had the force of law.

After the large joint family, the caste provided social security, helping destitute members and providing for widows and orphans. A man expelled from his caste was also automatically expelled from his family, unless the whole family accompanied him in his social ostracism. He was lost to society and could only consort with the lowest of the low. Though he might sometimes retain some of his former wealth, he was isolated, a tree torn up by the roots. Permanent loss of caste was the greatest catastrophe, short of death and the major chronic diseases, which could happen to a man.

Early Tamil literature gives no evidence of caste, but the growth of Aryan influence and the development of a more complex political and economic structure produced a system in some ways more rigid than that of the North. By the Cola period an important feature of South Indian Caste structure had appeared which has survived to the present day. In the Dravidian country families claiming to be Kshatriyas were few, other than the ruling families and Vysyas were equally rare. In the Dravidian country vysyas were rare. Nearly the whole of the population were brahmans, sudras or untouchables and the sudra castes which formed the mass of the people, were divided into two great caste groups, known as the right and left hands. The great animosity and rivalry which still exists between these groups is at least a thousand years old. On the right are the trading castes, some weaving castes, musicians, potters, washermen, barbers and most of the cultivating and labouring castes; on the left are various castes of craftsmen, such as weavers and leather workers, cowherds and some cultivating castes. We have no evidence of how this strange bisection of society arose.

Hypergamy never wholly disappeared. In Malabar, where matrilinear succession has continued almost to modern times, men of the great Brahman caste of Nambudiris have regularly married the women of the dominant secular caste, the Nayyars. In Bengal the Radhi caste of brahmans and the important and respectable castes of scribes (*kayastha*) and doctors (*vaidya*) are divided into sub-castes, which are hypergamous. The system is known as "kullinism", from the name of the highest sub-caste of the brahmans (*kulina*); It was by tradition imposed by the Bengal king Villala Sena (12th century), but is no doubt a survival from much earlier times.

The organisation of the castes independent of the government and with social ostracism as its most severe sanction, was a powerful factor in the survival of Hinduism. The Hindu, living under an alien political order imposed from above, retained his cultural individuality largely through his caste, which received most of the loyalty elsewhere felt towards king, nation and city. Caste was so strong that all attempts at breaking it down, until recent years, have ended in failure. Equalitarian religious reformers of the late Middle Ages, such as Basava, Raman and and Kabir, tried to abolish caste among their followers; but their sects soon took on the characteristics of new castes and in some cases divided into castes within themselves. The Sikhs, despite the outspoken sentiments of their gurus and the adoption of rites deliberately intended to break down caste prejudice, such as the ritual meal eaten in common did not overcome caste feeling. Even the Muslims for all their equalitarian faith, formed caste groups. The Syrian Christians of Malabar early divided into sections which took on a caste character, and when in the 16th century Roman Catholic missionaries began to make converts in South India their flocks brought their caste prejudices with them, and high caste converts held themselves aloof from those of the lower orders.

Only in the last fifty years has the caste system shown real signs of breaking down, thanks to the many inventions of the West not designed for use in a society divided into watertight compartments, the spread of Western education, growing national sentiment and the intensive propaganda of enlightened leaders. The process is not yet complete and it will be many years before all trace of caste feeling is eradicated; but when Mahatma Gandhi, in many ways socially conservative, persuaded his followers to sweep their own floors and clean their own latrines he sounded the death knell of the old Hindu social order, which, for all its faults, has preserved the identity of Indian society over centuries of foreign domination.

The abolition of Untouchability in all its forms, and making its practice a cognizable offence, was a far-reaching, but necessary, step in the fight against inequality. Only an indigenous government could have taken this radical step, and not an alien one. Of course, the legal abolition of Untouchability needs to be distinguished from its actual disappearance, particularly in the village. To take a few basic instances, it is a matter of common knowledge that even though the Scheduled Castes have the legal right to enter high caste temples, that right is not generally translated into practice. Any move on their part to enter caste Hindu temples would bring down the wrath of the high, particularly, the dominant castes. The Scheduled Castes are not allowed to draw water from the wells of the caste Hindus. Officials and politicians find it more convenient to get separate wells dug for the Scheduled Castes. In rural teashops the latter are nowadays served tea and snacks, but often in utensils meant exclusively for them. In other words, inequality continues but the Scheduled Castes have access to basic facilities which they did not have before. Yet another fact is relevant here; Pollution ideas have become weaker everywhere, even in villages, making social life easier than what it was before Independence. This is part of the wider phenomenon of increasing secularization.

The abolition of Untouchability is also backed up by certain positive measures devised for the advancement of the Scheduled Castes and Tribes. It may be noted here that the Scheduled Castes for purposes of the various benefits and concessions subsumed under the policy of "protective discrimination". But there is also lower level of protection that is accorded to the "Other Backward Classes" comprising certain socially, educationally and economically backward castes, identified primarily by each State government as needing special facilities and concessions in order to catch up with the more "advanced" sections of the population. Needless to say, the list varies from State to State, and some States, particularly the southern States, are more active in providing special facilities to the Other Backward Classes than the others. The "weaker sections" of the people subsuming the Scheduled Castes and Scheduled tribes as well as the Other Backward Classes, constitute, very roughly, a little over half the population. In other words, no other country in the world, poor or rich, is pursuing economic development while at the same time providing special facilities for such a large section of its population.

[**Source:** Adopted from the material "*The Wonder That Was India*" authored by A.L. Basham.]

The concessions and facilities, including reservation of seats in the lower houses of legislatures, and jobs in the government, proportionate to their numbers, provided for the Scheduled Castes and Tribes under the Constitution, are mandatory in nature. They were meant initially for a period of ten years, but have been renewed decennially by Parliament.

Reservation of seats in legislatures, originally intended to cover the federal Parliament and the State legislatures, has been extended to include local self-government (Panchayat Raj) bodies. Similarly, reservation of jobs in the government includes also the public sector concerns, which under the socialist ideology of the government, has expanded enormously.

Indeed, representation of members of the Scheduled Castes and Tribes is extended as a matter of routine to all government-appointed committees. Preference is also given to them in the allotment of surplus agricultural land – surplus obtained by imposing ceilings on rich farmers generally from the high castes —, in the allotment of free house sites, in the provision of modest housing, in the grant of loans by the nationalized banks for various self-help schemes and indeed, in every scheme devised for the benefit of the "weaker sections". The privileges enjoyed by the Scheduled Castes have earned them the envy of the higher castes who sarcastically refer to them as "government Brahmins" or the "new Brahmins". Cynical remarks are often heard that the government has only reversed the traditional caste system in the name of socialism. The Scheduled Tribes manage to escape such criticism because they live in compact blocks in the forested hills, isolated from the others. Also while they are poor and backward, they were not regarded as untouchable by the high castes.

The numerous measures devised for the benefit of the Scheduled Castes have resulted in a situation where atleast some groups among them, such as the Chamars of U.P., and the Mahars of Maharashtra, have improved their living conditions, perhaps more than some caste groups just above the untouchability line. The latter have suffered for the reason that the benefits earmarked for the Other Backward Classes are often collared by the educationally more advanced and numerically stronger amongst them, to the disadvantage of the other groups. That was why, for instance, the Nagan Gowda Committee, appointed by the Government of Karnataka in 1960 to examine the position of the Other Backward Classes in the State, recommended that the latter be divided into "backward" and "more backward" divisions, in order to assure the latter of a share of the benefits. At about the same time, a Kerala committee made a similar recommendation for the local backward classes. Backwardness is a relative phenomenon, both between castes and within each caste category and that is why its removal presents such an intractable problem.

[**Source**: "*viertel jahres berichte*" Probleme der international Zusammenarbeit – Problems of International Cooperation; Nr. 110 – December 1987.]

CHAPTER 3

A General Picture of the Dalits in India

The Scheduled Castes who are now known as Dalits constitute the majority under the BPL (Below Poverty Line). When we are speaking of clinical approach to rural development there is a need to understand the present status·and the dire needs of these poor segments of the population. We cannot simply think of the Dalits as a numerical number, but one has to understand their social history and their psychology when attempts are made to better their lives.

Dalits in India numbering around 800 distinguished groups who go by several ethnic names and titles constitute about 17% in India's population. Their lives in millennia have been poignant psycho-and social-suffocation. The discrimination meted out to them, the humiliation they have suffered for centuries, the hardship they have endured, the servitude they were subjected to and their earlier deep pathos of life runs into volumes. Even today despite constitutional and legislative safeguards and measures providing them some reservations and extending to them incentives exclusively, they have not wriggled out of their psychic social feeling of subordination and sense of inferiority.

Excepting in a few cases, the majority of the so-called higher caste Hindus appear to be reluctant and unwilling to treat the Dalits with equal respect and extend help to them and also see that assistance reaches them. Because of the long discriminatory tradition, a large number of higher caste groups appear not psychologically prepared to accept the Dalits as equals and extend help to them to bring them up to the level of the better off people. On the other hand the Dalits also make hesitant moves. One can find the pattern of behaviour among the elder generation and the younger generation in case of Dalits as well as non-Dalits. One could see today the younger generation among the Dalits, as a retaliatory measure to the past-untold discrimination meted out to their generations of ancestors, is demanding and aggressive in their behaviour. The only analogy to the turmoils undergone by the Dalits is the institution of slavery perpetrated by the white settlers in America.

Here it is relevant and interesting to have a comprehensive and yet brief anthropological account of Dalits in India. The statistical data relate to 1981 census.

The details furnished below cover 751 communities and their segments. Many Scheduled Castes have plural identifies and for an anthropologist the task of listing and studying them poses a dilemma. None of the identities can be ignored, for some of them may be transitory, but a majority is permanent. Indeed the plural identities of these people are largely due to the processes of fission and fusion that plagued the Indian caste system and the reform movements that have changed community names many times over. In retrospect and in the final analysis it is to be believed that every identity has a specificity to itself which is not traceable in another identity. Adi Andhra and Mala are not synonymous, nor Adi Dharmi and Chamar. In some cases, certain communities with similar names and even spelling were treated separately for their distinct cultural features and occupational diversity, such as the Kadaiyan from Kerala and Tamil Nadu, and the Turi from Gujarat and other places. The size of scheduled-caste communities is an important factor. Some of these communities consist of more than a million people, whereas others number fewer than 1000 persons. Out of the total population of the scheduled castes in the country, their largest concentration is in Uttar Pradesh (22.39 %), followed by West Bengal (11.46%), Bihar (9.68 %), Tamil Nadu (8.48 %), Andhra Pradesh (7.60%), Madhya Pradesh (.7.02%), Rajasthan (5.57%), Karnataka (5.34%), Maharashtra (4.28%), Punjab (4.31%), Orissa (3.69%), Haryana (2.35%), Gujarat (2.33%), Delhi

(1.07%), and in the remaining states/union territories their proportion is less. The smallest number of scheduled castes is found in Mizoram (135 persons). The scheduled caste communities perceive themselves mostly as local and regional communities. One hundred and five communities (13.8%) perceive their distribution at national level.

The scheduled caste communities are non-vegetarian except such sections of them as have been influenced by bhakti movements. The number of scheduled castes who are regular non-vegetarians is 404 (53.8%). A number of them consume cow beef – 104 communities (13.8%), whereas 117 communities (15.6%) consume ox beef; others eat pork (358 communities, 47.7%) and carrion (27 communities, 3.6%). Meat is their source of protein. Eighty-nine per cent of the communities reportedly consume milk. In all these communities alcoholic drinks are occasionally consumed; by men in 457 and by women in 284 communities. These alcoholic drinks are purchased mainly from the market, as only 20.8% take home brewed drinks. The transition from non-vegetarian to vegetarian food habits is observed among 101 communities. The incidence of beef-eating has gone down. With the rise in family income there is a marked increase in the consumption of fruits (18.2%), pulses 35.8%) and vegetables (39.9%).

Divisions also exist in terms of sub-castes or subgroups (178 communities) in the case of major scheduled castes. Differentiation among the subgroups is reported at social (428 communities), occupational (125) and religious (63) levels. Stratification has emerged with the rise of elites who have benefited from developmental programmes. Polarization and inequality have increased among various strata of the scheduled castes.

Scholars hold the view that the scheduled castes generally lie outside the chaturvarna system (avarnas). There is the Panchama cluster of communities in Andhra Pradesh who consider themselves the fifth varna. A number of scheduled castes do not recognize or place themselves within the varna system, particularly in Andhra Pradesh, Tamil Nadu, Karnataka, Kerala, Madhya Pradesh and Goa. In Maharashtra and Rajasthan between 25 to 33 per cent do not recognize varna. However, the data also suggest that a substantial number of scheduled caste people (80.2%) are aware of the four-fold varna system and a substantial number of them (70.2%) even place themselves within it. About 70.2 per cent recognize themselves as Sudra, 7.6 per cent as Kshatriyas. This corresponds by and large to the self-perception of scheduled castes. For example, 72.2 per cent of the scheduled castes perceive themselves as occupying low, 23.2 per cent as middle, and 4.4 per cent as high positions. Other communities see 91.2 per cent of the scheduled castes as occupying low, 7.9 per cent as middle and 0.3 per cent as high positions. This shows the very long way that the scheduled castes have to go in achieving a measure of equality with others and in getting their equal status recognized. A large number of scheduled castes are endogamous (96.3%). The incidence of hypergamy and hypogamy is negligible.

The women among the scheduled castes have a role in all economic and income generation activities, as well as in social functions (89.1%) and ritual matters (89.5 %). But they have generally a lower status (73%), and only a few have decision-making powers. The traditional institutions of social control are fairly active in as many as 82 per cent of the communities. The scheduled-caste communities are substantially represented in statutory panchayats which have come into existence. The traditional caste councils decide social matters and impose punishment for crimes and offences like adultery, elopement, disputes over land and water, disrespect for traditional norms, etc.

The scheduled castes are mainly landless (69.6%), with little control over resources such as land, forest and water. However, the distribution of land among them, besides other factors, has led to an increase in the number of landholders (28.5%). There has been a marked rise in the number of agricultural labourers (49.1%), casual labourers (72 %), industrial labourers (17.3%), plantation (6.1%) and fishing labour (2.5%). Child labour exists in 58.7% of the communities. Unlike the scheduled tribes, the scheduled caste-communities have followed a wide range of traditional occupations, usually more than one. Many of these, however, are rapidly disappearing. Prominent among the traditional occupations are skin and hide work, carrying carcasses, scavenging, drum-beating, playing music and singing. There were also acrobats like the Bazigar, magicians like the Bhanumati, devil dancers and exorcists like the Nalkadaya, the Pambada and the Malayan. The Bangali in Haryana and a few adjoining states, and the Garudi, were snake charmers, while the Baori prepared mohra (seal) and the Sindhuria manufactured vermilions. The Barar and the Kunchi Korava made combs for pit looms and the latter also did fibre-twinning to make ropes for peasants. The Mangan and the Turi are genealogists and bards. Some communities, like the Beda Jangam, the Kuruvan, etc., were soothsayers while the Singhiwala eked out a livelihood with their skills in traditional medicine. The Dhoba in many states of north India and the Velan and the Mannan in the south are washermen.

Service to the village community was rendered by the women of a few communities, like the Hari, who acted as midwives. Some communities, like the Bhand, earned money by mimicry. The Sindhollu of Andhra Pradesh lived by performing street drams (veedhibhagavatamulu) based on mythologies of the great tradition, and the Sillekyata by performing leather picture shows. The Gandhila were horse and ass traders, while the Sauntia were animal breeders. Communities like the Byagara, the Thoti, etc., were traditionally village servants, and the Kotegar guarded forts in olden days. The Bhoi, the Keot, the Kahar and a few others were palanquin-bearers. The Bindla of Andhra Pradesh had a role in the traditional system of invoking and appeasing village deities. Communities like the Darai and the Patni are traditionally ferrymen. A scheduled caste by name, the Kanda of Tripura supplied flowers to the royal palace (which then existed). An analysis of the occupations among scheduled castes suggests that some occupations like leatherwork, scavenging, etc., were considered degrading. However, in some areas certain groups are considered untouchable, whereas the same occupational groups are not considered so in other areas. If fishing communities are untouchable in eastern India, it is not the case in the western coastal areas or in the south except for the Bharatar of Tamil Nadu. The potters of Madhya

Pradesh or Manipur are untouchables, but not in any other area. The washermen in Andhra Pradesh are not untouchable, whereas in many other areas they are, and there they are notified as scheduled castes.

With the degradation of the environment and the depletion of forests there has been a sharp decline in many of the traditional economic activities of the scheduled castes (represented by percentages), such as hunting and gathering (43.86%), the trapping of birds and animals (17.64%) and shifting cultivation (20%). There has been a considerable involvement in modern occupations like horticulture (50%), settled cultivation (31.92%) and terrace cultivation (13.64%). However, there also has been a sharp rise in animal husbandry (32.84%) and wage labour (43.62%). There is increased involvement in activities like business (79.82%), trade (65.84%) and small-scale industry, which is reported from 23 communities. There is a phenomenal rise in white-collar employees (399 communities) and in private service (324) and self-employment (443). There has been a perceptible decline of crafts like dyeing (11.12%), weaving (9.28%), salt making (33.34%), weapon-making (33.35%), and metal work (10%). Specialized categories practicing the traditional occupations mentioned above have also suffered. However, a category of skilled labourer has emerged, registering an increase of 64.04 per cent. There is increased involvement in woodwork (51.52 per cent).

Though untouchability has been abolished by law, the study shows the persistence of untouchability, particularly in rural areas, in relation to the exchange of water and food with communities considered to be higher in the social hierarchy, even though commensal norms have generally weakened. Scheduled castes in every region and area in the country have their own hierarchy which prohibits the acceptance and exchange of water and food. For a Mala, a Madiga is an untouchable, and for both of them a Thoti is an untouchable. For a Meghwal, a Regar and a Bhangi are untouchables, whereas among the later two the Bhangi is an untouchable. Even the subgroups in a larger generic category have these distinctions. Among the Chamars, the Jatav, the

Mochi, the Satnami and many others have their own sense of superiority. So, there are a few scheduled castes from whom the other scheduled-caste communities accept neither food nor water. However, the data on the exchange of food and water show that there is a substantial number of communities with whom such exchanges do take place. There are also many scheduled castes, particularly those comprising professionals, who are not considered untouchables and with whom an exchange of food and water takes place. Further, the data also show that 42.3 per cent of the communities have putative kinship relations across communities, and 79.8 per cent of the communities share water sources and crematoria (66.2 %) with other communities. Ninety-one per cent of them visit the same religious shrines. As many as 681 communities (90.7%) participate in the traditional festivals and festivities, and 132 scheduled castes (17.6 %) have a specific role to play in these festivals.

The education has made an impact and promoted mobility is evident from the fact that a class of public servants (250 communities), teachers (364), administrators (155) and entrepreneurs/businessmen (286) has emerged among them. Political leadership has emerged at the village (39.4%), regional (18.5%) and national (4.5%) levels. One of the features of the degraded social status of scheduled-caste people has been the role of myths which explained their lowly origin, and even rationalized it. But there has been a sea change in recent years in the perception by scheduled-caste people of themselves; a new sense of self-respect. Part of this is due to the sanskritization of those sections of these communities which abstained from drinking liquor, eating non-vegetarian food (especially beef and pork)- in fact non-vegetarianism of all kinds. This also involved giving up names which were considered derogatory and assuming names which were considered respectable, e.g., the Chuhras called themselves Balmiki, Lalbegi; the Chandals became Namasudras; the Julaha called themselves Kabirpanthis; the Mala and Madiga named themselves Adi Andhra; the Pallan and Parayan claimed to be Adi Dravida, the Holeyas in Karnataka are now Adi Karnataka; the Chamar and Chuhra, after conversion to Sikhism, called themselves Ramdasia.

A new strand in the self-perception of the scheduled castes are the Neo-Buddhists who stress their identity as members belonging to an order that stands outside the varna system. In fact theirs is a newfound sense of dignity in their identity as members of the scheduled castes *in situ* without associating themselves either with the sanskritization process or various protestant reformist movements. In fact a new sense of self-respect is in the air. The old myths which legitimized degradation are being discarded. Colonial ethnographic surveys were replete with stories of degradation caused by beef-eating and that arising out of functions such as removing carcasses. These are either being ignored now or are referred to very weakly. Instead there is a new sense of dignity and self-assertion symbolized by Dalit literature. The Dalits now not only question the varna system and the ideology underlying it but consider their movement a larger struggle for equality. In this respect they have not only continued with Babasaheb B.R. Ambedkar's struggle for equality and self-respect but have taken it into new areas. The new leadership has articulated a radical counter-ideology, powerfully expressed in a burst of creative writings. The Dalit sahitya is in vibrant form today. The Dalit poetry states the stark truth and calls upon Dalits to act:

As mentioned earlier, the Scheduled Castes are a heterogeneous category. Most of the sections of the scheduled castes have generally lived in symbiosis with other sections of the general population. They have been, and are being, closely integrated with the country's larger society. This fact, and this process, is also reflected in economy, culture and politics.

The Madiga of Andhra Pradesh are also referred to as Arundhatiya, Jambavalu, Jambhavanthulu, Adi-Andhra, etc. There are many legendary accounts of the origin of the Madiga. The Madiga and Mala have common legends that speak of their origins. Many legends say that the divine cow, Kamadhenu, was killed by two watchmen of Eswara and as a consequence they were cursed by him. The descendants of these two watchmen were the Madiga and Mala. Most Madigas live in their own hamlets (Madiga Palle) segregated from the main village. According to the 1981 census, the population of the Madiga in Andhra Pradesh is 3,572,072. They are predominantly found in rural areas. However, a considerable number of them, i.e., 477,596 persons (13.37 per cent of the total population) are returned from urban areas. The Dravidian language, Telugu and the Telugu script are used for both intra-and inter-group communication. The morphometric features of the Madiga in Andhra Pradesh fall between the tribal communities and the agricultural and economically dominant castes and, in general, are similar to the average physical features of the state's population. The Madiga are predominantly round-headed, of below medium to short height and have a broader facial profile. They show a higher occurrence of gene B (27-35 per cent) than gene A (13-14 percent). In the Tirupati area they were found to have an excess of gene O (73 per cent) than in the north-western parts of A.P. (61 per cent). The presence of Sickle cell trait, low levels of Hp^1 allele, relatively low levels of Rh-negative cases (4 %) and low frequency of colour-blind males, indicate their similarity with tribal groups of the area. The Madiga are non-vegetarian and they are in the habit of taking alcoholic drinks frequently. It is stated that their untouchable status was due to their habit of eating beef. Rice is the staple cereal consumed.

MALAS

Malas are settled in every Andhra village and constitute the backbone of the agricultural labour force. Out of their total population, 49.59% are returned as workers (58.50% males and 40.44 % females). Of them, 67.64 % are returned as agricultural labourers, whereas only 18.41% are cultivators; 1.10% of the workers are engaged in livestock and forestry. The remaining 12.85 % of the workers are engaged in various other services. Intercommunity linkages between the Malas and the other communities are characteristically limited to the economic sphere. Of late, particularly in urban areas, there has been an increasing interaction between the Mala and other caste communities in terms of exchange of food and water. Many changes of greater importance can be witnessed among the Malas in their socio-economic life, mainly due to the government's interventionist and protective developmental programmes. They avail of all the facilities extended to them for the improvement of their quality of life. There has been considerable progress in the field of education. Their literacy rate, according to the 1981 census, is 21.23%. The sexwise literacy rates for male and female, according to the 1981 census, are 29.72 % and 12.51%, respectively.

At present, some Malas are employed as clerks, administrators, doctors, engineers, teachers and defence personnel. They forge and establish intercommunity links at various levels, though only in a limited way. Some of them have improved their economic condition by availing of different developmental programmes. Their literacy rate is only 12.75% (1981 census). The Mala in the Union Territory of Pondicherry call themselves Adi Andhra and are distributed all over Yanam. Their population, including Mala Masti, in Pondicherry, according to the 1981 census, is only 11. It appears that in the 1981 census, they mainly returned themselves as Adi Andhra who numbered 2148. In addition to their mother tongue, Telugu, they are conversant in Tamil. As Pondicherry was a colony of the French, the elderly people of the community can understand and speak French. The script commonly used for writing is Tamil. In terms of food habits, social division and customs, they do not show much variation.

NEO-BUDDHIST (NAV BUDDHIST)

Also referred to as Nav Buddhist, they are the new converts to Buddhism. Baba Saheb Ambedkar initiated these conversions to the Buddhist faith and the first conversion took place in 1956 at Nagpur in Maharashtra. Dr. Ambedkar believed that only by leaving the Hindu fold could the depressed castes free themselves from the burden of untouchability. Conversions have since taken place in different states. A large-scale conversion took place in 1981, the silver jubilee year of the first conversion, when a large number of Jatavs in Uttar Pradesh were converted to Buddhism. Neo-Buddhists are distributed all over the country, but they are largely concentrated in Maharashtra, Uttar Pradesh, Karnataka, Gujarat, Andhra Pradesh and Punjab. In Uttar

Pradesh, most of them live in Bareilly, Badaun, Moradabad and Agra districts. The Hindi language and the Devanagari script are used for both inter-group and intra-group communication. They are occasionally non-vegetarians. Of late, there has been a shift to vegetarianism.

Neo-Buddhists use surnames like Gautam, Bodh and Ashok for boys and Gautami for females. Marriages are contracted within the community beyond blood relations. The usual form of marriage is monogamy, and adult marriage is the norm. Glass bangles, the vermilion mark, toe-rings, etc., are the marriage symbols for women. There is no dowry. After marriage, the patrilocal rule of residence is followed. Divorce is not permissible. However, levirate and sororate are permissible. They usually live in nuclear families. Inheritance is in the male line and the eldest son succeeds to the familial authority. Their women share the tasks of bringing potable water, collecting fuel and fodder and assisting their men in agricultural operations. Besides, they are also proficient in embroidery. A pre-delivery ritual known as *gabb-mangal* is performed, in which panchsheel is adopted and a bhikshu recites the dhammapada and performs the jai mangal asthagatha. The bhikshu or bodh acharya names the infants. The first feeding of cereals (*annaprasan*) is performed at the age of five months. The tonsure ceremony (*keshkampan*) is initiated by a bhikshu but the Nai is given cash and grains for performing the tonsure. The ear-piercing ceremony (*karan vichedan*) and initiation to education (*vidhya arambh*) are performed at the age of five years. The religious course of prabajya is taken by both married and unmarried persons. The jal kriya or samarpan rituals have replaced kanyadan and haldi is performed three days prior to the marriage. The marriage is solemnized at the bride's place. The important marriage rituals are oathtaking, panchsheel, jal kriya and jai mangal asthagatha. Marriages are registered with the Bhartiya Bodh Parishad. On death (parinirvan), the corpse is either cremated or buried. On the fifth day after death, the paaritrana path is performed.

In addition to their traditional occupation of shoe making and leatherwork, they are also engaged in sharecropping as well as wage labour. Nowadays, some of them are employed in government and private services and a few of them are in industry.

The Bharatiya Bodh Parishad to which their community is affiliated takes care of their social disputes. They believe in the original granth, Tripitak. A bhikshu performs their different life-cycle rituals. They observe the general festivals of the Buddhists and also celebrate the birth and death anniversaries of Baba Saheb Ambedkar. They are experts in shoe making and in embroidery on cloth and leather.

Traditional intercommunity linkages with the different untouchable communities are still maintained. They share the same water sources and cremation grounds with other communities. They continue to cultivate the fields of upper caste Hindus as sharecroppers and also work for them as labourers. The scholars, teachers, doctors, engineers and administrators from amongst them promote modern intercommunity linkages. Some of them have emerged as political leaders at the national level.

The Adi Hindu Movement which propounded the theory that the untouchables are the original inhabitants of India did not find favour with the Arya Samaj and its followers like the Jatav, some of whom identify themselves to be Nav Buddhists. In Swami Atma Ram's *Gyan Samudra* it was mentioned that according to Lomash Ramayana found in Nepal, the Jatav race was traced to a gotra of Lord Shiva. Thus, it was stated that the Jatav are Kshatriyas. Now after their conversion to Buddhism in 1956, they have begun to assert that they are indigenes of the soil, who were once Buddhists before they adopted Hinduism after Aryan migration.

Their attitude towards formal education is partly favourable for both boys and girls. For curing their ailments, they use both modern and indigenous medicare systems. Their attitude towards family planning is positive and they have adopted modern methods of family planning. They make use of irrigation and electricity facilities. Their children avail of the midday-meal scheme in schools. Their attitude towards saving is encouraging.

In Karnataka, most of the Neo-Buddhists are converts from Mahar, Chalvadi, Holeya and Madiga communities. They are largely concentrated in Bangalore, Mysore, Tumkur, Bidar, Gulbarga, Dharwad, Belgaum and Kolar districts. The different linguistic groups speak their respective languages at home and use Kannada for inter-group communications. The Kannada script is used. They are non-vegetarians who consume beef and pork. Rice, wheat and jowar are their staple cereals and tur is the main pulse consumed. Their men occasionally consume alcoholic drinks purchased from the market. Smoking beedis and cigarettes and chewing betel leaf are common habits that are encountered amongst them.

They place themselves in the Sudra category of the chaturvarna system. Marriage with one's father's sister's daughter, mother's brother's daughter or elder sister's daughter is permissible. Adult marriage is the norm and marriage is arranged through negotiation. The thali and toe-rings are the marriage symbols for women. Monogamy is the form of marriage. Divorce is not permitted, but widow and widower remarriage is allowed. Vertically extended families are predominant, however there has been a decline in the number of extended families. Their women participate in economic activities like agricultural operations and animal husbandry, besides participating in social, ritual and religious spheres. Birth pollution lasts for eleven days. A few of them observe the initiation ceremony (sila) which is related to the observance of the five principles of Buddhism, i.e., panch sheel (abstention from killing, stealing, adultery, telling lies and drinking of liquor). Puberty rites (pushpavati) are performed on menarche. Marriages are solemnized at the bridegroom's house. The marriage ritual starts with an exchange of garlands followed by the tying of the thali to the bride by the bridegroom. The marriage feast is hosted by the bridegroom's parents. The dead are either buried or cremated and death pollution is observed. On the sixteenth day after death, a mortuary rite known as tithi is performed. Ancestor worship is observed.

In Andhra Pradesh, Dr. Ambedkar's teachings have inspired several communities, which have converted to

Buddhism. They are now called Neo-Buddhists and are found in Visakhapatnam, East Godavari and West Godavari districts. They speak Telugu and use the Telugu script. They recite the Panchasheel and Trisaran in the Pali language during the puja. The Neo-Buddhists are non-vegetarian. Their personal names are suffixed with Gautam, Buddha, Vikas, Ashok, etc. Sometimes they are also named after characters in Buddhist literature. They are largely drawn from various scheduled castes like the Mala, Madiga, etc., who, after their conversion, do not strictly follow the earlier caste distinctions. They follow surname (intiperu) exogamy and marry either the mother's brother's daughter or the father's sister's daughter. Sororal polygyny exists among them. Their women wear a thali (mangalasutra), vermilion (kankanam) and toe-rings (Mettelu) as marriage symbols. They follow patrilocal residence after marriage. Divorce is not permissible, but widow and widower remarriage is permissible. The majority of their families are of the nuclear type. All the male children inherit an equal share of the ancestral property. The eldest son succeeds as the head of the family. Women have a role in socio-religious functions and claim to have a secondary status. The tonsure ceremony is performed in the ninth month of the child. Puberty rites (Mangalasnanam) are performed for girls. Marriage rituals take place at the bridegroom's house or at Buddha viharas. A Bhikshu or an Upasak imparts Trisaran and Panchasheel to the bride and the groom before a picture of Lord Buddha. Then their names are registered in the Bharatiya Bodh Parishad. They either cremate or bury the dead. Death pollution is observed for five days. They do not perform ancestor worship.

Agricultural labour is the main occupation of the Neo-Buddhists. Some of them work as daily-wage labourers at construction sites, factories, etc., and a few other are employed as doctors, lawyers, teachers, etc., in government establishments. The Buddhist Sangam settles their disputes. The elderly monks of the Neo-Buddhists follow the Mahayana sect of Buddhism. After their conversion, they started observing Buddha Jayanti or Buddha Poornima, Ambedkar's birth and death anniversaries and Vijaya Dasami (Dussehra). Vijaya Dasami is specially observed because Dr. Ambedkar embraced Buddhism on that day. They have their own Bhikshu to conduct socio-religious functions. A fast is observed on full-moon days, as Buddha was born, received enlightenment and died, i.e., attained Mahaparinirvana on a full-moon day (Poornima). They accept food and water from all Hindu castes. The Brahman, Kshatriya and Vaishya communities accept only sidha food from them. In Andhra Pradesh, the Hindus do not treat them as equals in spite of their conversion to Buddhism. They receive the services of a barber (Mangali) and washerman (Chakali). They have their own viharas where religious teaching is imparted. They share public amenities like cremation/burial grounds and schools with other communities. Their attitude towards the formal education of their boys and girls is positive. Modern methods of family welfare are being adopted. They are also availing of financial assistance from institutions like the Andhra Pradesh State Financial Corporation and from banks. Since 1990, the government has extended the facility of reservation in jobs to the scheduled-caste converts to Buddhism.

PANCHAMA

The term Panchama means the fifth one, alluding to a non-existent fifth varna. All these groups later came to be called Harijans, scheduled castes and Dalits. It is often pointed out that the Panchama include many other groups. Panchama should be regarded as a varna, because Manu declared that there could never be a fifth varna. Panchama is, in fact, a generic term encompassing different endogamous groups. These are further subdivided by surnames (intiperu). The surnames, besides being exogamous groups, are also meant to indicate descent and ancestry. They also place themselves above the Jambavulu and below the Brahman, Raju, Komati, Kapu, Setti Balija, Gowda and Golla. Some of them consider themselves Sudras in the chaturvarna order. Group endogamy and surname exogamy are the general marriage rules observed. The Panchama are largely landless and only a few own cultivable land ranging from half an acre to five acres. Traditionally, they are agricultural labourers. Toddy-tapping, plucking coconuts, government service, cycle-rickshaw-pulling, etc., are the other occupations tht are pursued. According to the 1981 census, 51.07 per cent of them are workers (62.81% males and 39.13% females). Of them, a majority are agricultural labourers (71.41%) and cultivators (9.57%). The rest (3.32%) are engaged in mining and quarrying, 2.35% in the household industries and 13.35% in other services.

PARAIYAN/PARAYAN

Bishop Caldwell is of the opinion that the name Paraiyan is from the Tamil word parai, a drum, as certain paraiyans act as drummers at marriages, funerals, village festivals and on occasions when government or commercial announcements are proclaimed (Thurston, 1909).

Pulayan, along with the Izhavas and some other high-castes, participated in the Vaikom Satyagraha, which was started in 1924. In 1907, they started the Sadhu Jana Paripalana Sangham (SJPS) and Pulaya Mahasabha. In Perinad in Quilon district, the Pulayan began a movement against the traditional practice of their women wearing bead necklaces, which was considered a sign of degradation. This was strongly resented by the Nairs. Finally, the Pulayan women won the right to throw away the beads.

SANTIA

Distributed in Kota and Jhalawar districts of Rajasthan, the Santia are a migrant community from Raipur district in Madhya Pradesh. They are notified as Santia, Satia and their population, according to the 1981 census, is 5372. They are a predominantly rural-based community and more than 91 per cent of their total population is returned from rural areas. They speak the Indo-Aryan language, Gujarati, among themselves and Hindi is spoken with others. The Devanagari script is used. Both male and female wear a ceramic bead necklace. They are non-vegetarian and consume beef, pork and carrion. Their staple cereals are Jowar and Maize. Alcoholic drinks, purchased from the market, are occasionally consumed. There are both Hindu and Muslim segments among them. The former do not practice consanguinity whereas the later does. Village exogamy and monogamy are the marriage rules observed.

SAPELA / SAPERA

Known as Sapela, Sapad or Sapera, they are snake charmers. The word Sapera is derived from sap, meaning snake. Rose (1919) mentions Sapela, Sapera or Sipada as a snake-catcher, like the Sapela. The Sapela or Sampela claim to be an offshoot of the Jogi. They are distributed all over Haryana and their population, according to the 1981 census, is 4716 (2722 males and 1994 females) and they are primarily rural-based community. They are also returned from Punjab, Himachal Pradesh, Delhi and Chandigarh. In different parts of Haryana they use the Indo-Aryan language, Haryanvi, for both inter- and intra-group communication. The Devanagari script is used,. Their staple food constitutes pulse (dal), unleavened wheat bread (roti) and vegetable (sabzi). They prefer wheat to rice. They are more or less regular non-vegetarian and occasionally consume alcoholic drinks. The income generating activities are snake-charming, selling of snake venom and rearing mules for sale. To supplement the family income, they play on a gourd-pipe and dance in marriage parties. According to the 1981 census, 15.92 per cent of their total population (25.94% male and 2.26 % female) is returned as workers. Out of them 13.59 per cent are engaged in manufacturing, processing, etc. and 41.41 per cent are in other services which include workers engaged in playing on the gourd-pipe and those who dance in marriage parties. However, a considerable number of them, i.e., 39.28 per cent, are returned as agricultural labourers, 2.53 per cent as cultivators and 3.19 per cent as engaged in various other services.

While the study undertaken by the Anthropological Survey of India has covered the scheduled castes above a population of 10,000 in all the states and union territories of India, it has left twelve communities in a few states and one union territory, whose major components are listed below. These communities along with the state/union territory of their distribution, their population (1981 census) and an explanation for not studying them, are all appended below:

Sl.no.	Community	State / UT	Explanation
1.	**Ad Dharmi**	Himachal Pradesh (15,098)	Reported as a Synonym for Chamar
2.	**Adi Andhra**	Andhra Pradesh (698,857)	Being a Generic Group, Its Constituent Communities Have Been Studied.
3.	**Barahar, Basod**	Madhya Pradesh (60,789)	Studied as Basor in Madhya Pradesh
4.	**Bhangi**	Delhi (21,752)	Reported as a Synonym for Chuhra and Balmiki.
5.	**Chakkiliyan**	Kerala (29,001)	Studied as Arundhatiyar.
6.	**Holaya, Holer**	Maharashtra (14,927)	Reported as a Synonym for Holar
7.	**Kabir Panthi or Julaha**	Haryana (31,503)	Studied as Julaha.
8.	**Madari**	Tamil Nadu (346, 899)	Reported as a Synonym for Chakkiliyan.
9.	**Mala**	Maharashtra (11,890)	Reported to be Untraceable.
10.	**Mallah**	West Bengal (38,101)	Reported as a Synonym for Deshwali Majhi.
11.	**Moger**	Kerala (19,665)	'Real' Moger Are Untraceable.
12.	**Pallan**	Tamil Nadu (993,070)	Studied as Kudumban.

CONCLUSION

The details of data that are provided above would, it is believed, help the development agencies and the change agents in the field to understand and recognize the way to go about extending help to bring the Dalits to the surface, to the level of other groups who would enjoy respect, recognition and politico-economic advancement. Even though it may take several generations to bridge the gap but genuine attempts are to be pursued to do justice to the Dalits in terms of their overall development.

A list of those unstudied communities, whose population is below 10,000 along with the states and union territories where they were not studied, and their population figures (1981 census or as in the case of Assam, 1971 census) is appended below:

Sl.No.	Community	State / Union Territory and Population
1.	Adi Dharmi	Chandigarh (1431), Haryana (698), Rajasthan (780)
2.	Adi Andhra	Kerala (7353), Pondicherry (2148)
3.	Adi Dravida	Kerala (2458)
4.	Adi Karnataka	Kerala (1087)
5.	Ager	Gujarat (151), Maharashtra (3846)
6.	Agria	Delhi (1139)
7.	Ajila	Karnataka (1301), Kerala (155), Tamil Nadu (35)
8.	Arwa Mala	Karnataka (171), Maharashtra (241)
9.	Arunthathiyar	Karnataka (899)
10.	Audhelia	Orissa (15)
11.	Bagdi	Tripura (239)
12.	Baira	Tamil Nadu (431)
13.	Bakad, Bant	Gujarat (303), Maharashtra (736)
14.	Bakuda	Tamil Nadu (198)
15.	Bandhela	Himachal Pradesh (30)

(*contd.*)

Sl.No.	Community	State / Union Territory and Population
16.	Bandi	Kerala (24)
17.	Bangali	Chandigarh (49)
18.	Bansphor	Arunachal Pradesh (152), Meghalaya (212), Mizoram (8)
19.	Bantar	West Bengal (2086)
20.	Barar, Burar, Berar Barar, Burar, Berar	Haryana (957), Himachal Pradesh (416)Chandigarh (200)
21.	Basor, BurudBasor, Burud, Bansor, Bansodi, Bansphor, Basar	Orissa (178)Madhya Pradesh
22.	Bathada	Kerala (46)
23.	Batwal	Chandigarh (41), Haryana (524)
24.	Bauria, Bawaria Bauria or Bawaria	Himachal Pradesh (87)Chandigarh (791)
25.	Bavuri	Orissa (50)
26.	Bediya, Beriya	Rajsthan (2361)
27.	Bellara	Kerala (45), Tamil Nadu (44)
28.	Bhangi	Dadra and Nagar Haveli (44)
29.	Bhanjra	Chandigarh (207)
30.	Bharatar	Kerala (1892)
31.	Bhuinmali, Mali Bhinmali or Mali Bhuinmali or Mali	Meghalaya (201), Arunachal Pradesh (36), Mizoram (3)
32.	Bindla	Karnataka (194), Maharashtra (303), Meghalaya (303)
33.	Brittial-Bania or BaniaBrittial Bania, Bania	Arunachal Pradesh (102), Mizoram (2), Meghalaya (115)
34.	Byagara	Maharashtra (356)
35.	Chakkiliyan	Karnataka (2831)
36.	ChalavadiChalvadi, Channayya	Tamil Nadu (131), Gujarat (58)

(*contd.*)

Sl.No.	Community	State / Union Territory and Population
37.	Chamar, Muchi	Kerala (298), Tamil Nadu (165)
38.	Chambhar	Andhra Pradesh (520, Daman and Diu (22)
39.	Chanal	Chandigarh (90), Haryana (293), Punjab (139)
40.	Chandal	Rajasthan (1105)
41.	Chandala	Andhra Pradesh (184), Karnataka (175), Kerala (90), Tamil Nadu (37)
42.	Chaupal	West Bengal (37)
43.	Chenna Dasar, Holaya Dasar Chenna Dasar, Holaya Dasar, Holeya Dasari	Gujarat (139), Maharashtra (631)
44.	Chohra (Sweeper)	Delhi (3272)
45.	Dabgar	West Bengal (460)
46.	Dagi	Chandigarh (4), Haryana (50), Punjab (54)
47.	Dakkal, Dokkalwar	Karnataka (141), Maharashtra 342)
48.	Dandasi	Tripura (57)
49.	Darain	Chandigarh (23), Haryana (55), Himachal Pradesh (656)
50.	Dhanak	Himachal Pradesh (34)
51.	Dhaogri, Dhuai	Himachal Pradesh (793)
52.	Dhogri, Dhangri, SiggiDhogri, Dhangri or Siggi	Haryana (438), Punjab (265), Chandigarh (21)
53.	Dhor	Andhra Pradesh (2443)
54.	Dhor, Kakkayya, Kankayya	Gujarat (877)
55.	Dhupi or Dhobi Dhupi, Dhobi	Arunachal Pradesh (353), Mizoram (33), Meghalaya (313), Manipur (186)
56.	Domban	Tamil Nadu (8482)
57.	Dome, Dom	Rajasthan (3692)

(contd.)

Sl.No.	Community	State / Union Territory and Population
58.	Dum	Tripura (283)
59.	Dumna, Mahasha or DoomDumna, Mahasha, Doom	Chandigarh (112), Haryana (9248)
60.	Dosadha	Orissa (455)
61.	Dugla or Dholi Dugla, Dholi	Arunachal Pradesh (7), Mizoram (4), Meghalaya (22), Assam (4013)
62.	Gagra	Chandigarh (37), Haryana (58), Himachal Pradesh (6)
63.	Gandhila or Gandhil Gondola Gandhila, Gandil Gondola	Chandigarh (22), Himachal Pradesh (6)
64.	Garoda, Garo	Karnataka (1219), Maharashtra (352)
65.	Gharami	Uttar Pradesh (615)
66.	Ghasi	Tripura (443)
67.	Ghasi, Haddi, Relli Chachandi	Andhra Pradesh (1872)
68.	Godagali	Kerala (37), Orissa (24), Tamil Nadu (24)
69.	Godari	Orissa (225)
70.	Godda	Kerala (186)
71.	Gosangi	Karnataka (7474), Kerala (769), Tamil Nadu (157)
72.	Halalkhor	Bihar (5463), West Bengal (1348)
73.	Halleer	Gujarat (28)
74.	Halsar, Haslar, Hulasvar, Halasvar	Gujarat (154), Maharashtra (123)
75.	Hari	Uttar Pradesh (2121)
76.	Hira	Arunachal Pradesh (9), Meghalaya (48), Mizoram(3)
77.	Holar, Valhar	Gujarat (170), Karnataka (1190)
78.	Holaya, HolerHoleya	Gujarat (92),Andhra Pradesh (664)
79.	Holeya Dasari	Andhra Pradesh (620)

(*contd.*)

Sl.No.	Community	State / Union Territory and Population
80.	Jaggali	Karnataka (229), Tamil Nadu (1248)
81.	Jalkeot	Arunachal Pradesh (34), Meghalaya (8), Mizoram (2)
82.	Jambuvulu	Karnataka (4082), Pondicherry (237)
83.	Jhalo, Malo, Jhalo-MaloJhalo, Malo or Jhalo-Malo	Meghalaya (1052), Arunachal Pradesh (75), Mizoram (1)
84.	Jolaha	Jammu and Kashmir (371)
85.	Kabir Panthi	Delhi (4334)
86.	Kadaiyan	Karnataka (172)
87.	Kaibartta or Jaliya	Arunachal Pradesh (764), Mizoram (6)
88.	Kakkalan	Tamil Nadu (66)
89.	Kalladi	Karnataka (511), Tamil Nadu (409)
90.	Kanakkan, Padanna	Tamil Nadu (176)
91.	Kanjar	West Bengal (1067)
92.	Karimpalan	Tamil Nadu (9)
93.	Katia, Patharia	Maharashtra (3207)
94.	Kavara	Tamil Nadu 3711)
95.	Khangar, Kanera, Mirdha	Maharashtra (858)
96.	Koch	West Bengal (9714)
97.	Kooch-Band, Kuchband	Rajasthan (1509)
98.	Koosa	Kerala (268), Tamil Nadu 41)
99.	Kootan, Koodan	Tamil Nadu (147)
100.	Kori or Koli	Chandigarh (1889)
101.	Kotal	Tripura (43)
102.	Kudumban	Karnataka (140), Kerala (3368)
103.	Kurariar	West Bengal (1416)
104.	Lalbegi	Arunachal Pradesh (20), Assam (45), Delhi (134), Meghalaya (30), Mizoram (3)

(contd.)

Sl.No.	Community	State / Union Territory and Population
105.	Madari	Delhi (?), Karnataka (3434)
106.	Madiga	Orissa ((1314)
107.	MaharMahar, Taral, Dhegumegu	Dadra and Nagar Haveli (83), Rajasthan (7635)
108.	Mahara	Arunachal Pradesh (13), Assam (899), Mizoram (6), Meghalaya (Not available)
109.	Mahayavanshi Mahyavanshi, Dhed Mahyavanshi, Dhed, Dheda, Venkar, Maru Vankar Mahayanvashi, Dhed, Vankar, Maru Vankar	Goa (119), Dadra and Nagar Haveli (943), Rajasthan (1868), Karnataka (719)
110.	Maila	Tamil Nadu (47)
111.	Mazhabi	Himachal Pradesh (221)
112.	Mala, Jhala, Malo, Zala	Orissa (6118)
113.	Mala Dasari	Karnataka (2193)
114.	Mala Dasu	Andhra Pradesh (8384)
115.	Mala Jangam	Karnataka (291)
116.	Mala Masti	Karnataka (34), Maharashtra (60)
117.	Mala Sale, Netkani	Karnataka (21), Maharashtra (437)
118.	Mang	Goa (686), Daman and Diu (16), Orissa (273)
119.	Mang, Matang, Minimadig	Gujarat (2765), Rajasthan (241)
120.	Mang Garodi, Mang-GarudiMang Garudi, Mang Garodi Mang Garudi	Rajasthan (177), Karnataka (2339), Gujarat (1184)
121.	Mangan	Orissa (983)
122.	Manne	Karnataka (174), Maharashtra (1752)

(*contd.*)

Sl.No.	Community	State / Union Territory and Population
123.	Mavilan	Karnataka (51)
124.	Megh	Chandigarh (338)
125.	Meghwal Meghval, Menghvar	Delhi (1481), Karnataka (22)
126.	Mehtar or Bhangi Mehtar, Bhangi Mehtor	Arunachal Pradesh (209), Mizoram (10), Meghalaya (621), Orissa (2332), Tripura (1279)
127.	Mitha Ayyalvar	Maharashtra (202)
128.	Moger	Tamil Nadu (89)
129.	Muchi, Ravidas Muchi or Rishi Muchi, Rishi	Manipur (193), Arunachal Pradesh (328), Meghalaya (1204)
130.	Mukri	Gujarat (26), Maharashtra (74)
131.	Mundala	Andhra Pradesh (853), Tamil Nadu (26)
132.	Musahar	Orissa (29)
133.	Nadia, Hadi	Karnataka (118), Maharashtra (249)
134.	Nalakeyava	Karnataka (4928), Kerala (269), Tamil Nadu (7)
135.	Namasudra	Arunachal Pradesh (540), Manipur (2423), Meghalaya (1112), Mizoram (6)
136.	Nat Nat (Rana)	Chandigarh (21), Himachal Pradesh (232), Uttar Pradesh (?)Delhi (?)
137.	Nayadi	Karnataka (1434), Tamil Nadu (360)
138.	Od	Chandigarh (35)
139.	Padannan	Tamil Nadu (Not available)
140.	Paky	Pondicherry (42)
141.	Pallan	Karnataka (745)
142.	Palluvan	Tamil Nadu (151)
143.	Pambada Pambada, Pambanda	Tamil Nadu (624), Andhra Pradesh (2333)
144.	Pamidi	Orissa (64)

(contd.)

Sl.No.	Community	State / Union Territory and Population
145.	Panchama	Karnataka (785), Kerala (134), Orissa (269), Tamil Nadu (76)
146.	Panika	Orissa (?)
147.	Panniandi	Karnataka (97)
148.	Paraiyan, Paraya	Karnataka (2307)
149.	Pasi	Chandigarh (928), Gujarat (1164), Himachal Pradesh (226), Rajasthan (943)
150.	Pathiyan	Tamil Nadu (23)
151.	Patni	Arunachal Pradesh (11), Manipur (2293), Meghalaya (54), Mizoram (4)
152.	Perna	Chandigarh (18), Himachal Pradesh (21)
153.	Pherera	Chandigarh (12), Haryana (24)
154.	Pulaya Vettuvan	Kerala (1008)
155.	Puthirai Vannan	Kerala (280)
156.	Raneyar	Kerala (148), Tamil Nadu (4), Andhra Pradesh (1845)
157.	Samagara	Andhra Pradesh (1845), Tamil Nadu (37)
158.	Samban	Karnataka (71), Kerala (2486), Pondicherry (16)
159.	Sanbhai	Chandigarh (89)
160.	Sanhai	Haryana (59), Punjab (73)
161.	Sansi	Maharashtra (531)
162.	Sansoi	Chandigarh (138), Haryana (68), Punjab (32)
163.	Sapela	Chandigarh (138), Himachal Pradesh (23)
164.	Sarbhangi	Rajasthan (613)
165.	Sarera	Chandigarh (215), Haryana (51)
166.	Shenva, Chenva, Sedma, Ravat	Maharashtra (501)

(*contd.*)

Sl.No.	Community	State / Union Territory and Population
167.	Sidhollu, Chindollu	Karnataka (41), Maharashtra (181)
168.	Sirkiband	Chandigarh (178), Delhi (566), Himachal Pradesh (15)
169.	Sutradhar	Arunachal Pradesh (100), Manipur (11), Meghalaya (270), Mizoram (Not available),
170.	Tamadia	Orissa (238)
171.	Thoti	Karnataka (1184), Kerala (411)
172.	Tirgar, Tirbanda	Karnataka (173), Maharashtra (1154)
173.	Turi	Maharashtra (275), Rajasthan (2041)
174.	Vallon	Kerala (431), Tamil Nadu (104)
175.	Valluvan	Karnataka (1002)
176.	Velan	Tamil Nadu (318)
177.	Vetan	Pondicherry (307), Tamil Nadu (774)
178.	Vettuvan	Tamil Nadu (143)

Source: *The People of India*, The Scheduled Castes, National Series, Vol.II, edited by K.S.Singh, Anthropological Survey of India, Oxford University Press, Delhi, 1995.

CHAPTER 4

Functional Relationship of some Higher Caste Groups with Dalits (Male and Madiga) - A Case Study

We have what we may call differential social distance maintained by higher caste groups in respect to the Dalits. Even though there is no question of untouchability as it prevailed earlier in the case of Dalits, within the so called higher caste groups we find graded and differential social distance and communal relations maintained by them. Even among the non-Dalits some of them claim superior status, though the other groups consider them as lower to their own. These views and attitudes are varied each group claiming higher than the other. Whatever may be the caste dynamics and social distance maintained by higher castes, the whole realm of higher caste groups maintained social distance in respect to the Dalits. Since untouchability has been abolished constitutionally with gradual upliftment of Dalits through legal measures reservations in respect to education and employment changes are taking place on either side.

On one hand the Dalits are gaining strength and slowly moving forward and on the other hand the higher caste groups are coming down reducing the distance of interaction with the Dalits. This significant change on the part of the non-Dalits is to be largely attributed to their fear of meeting with the legal consequences, the moment they are found ill-treating the Dalits. It is to be pointed out that this kind of change on the part of the higher castes, largely as mentioned above is due to fear of legal consequences and problem of public opinion.

The way in which the Dalits have been treated all over the country is an open book. Even though every adult individual of both sex have full knowledge of the institution of caste and its functional ramifications, an attempt is made in order to understand the present kind of relationship between the higher caste groups and the Dalits.

To meet this need some 100 higher caste respondents were selected from the district of Kanyakumari in Tamil Nadu and Chittoor district in Andhra Pradesh. The analysis of 100 respondents is discussed below. The respondents belong to different caste groups.

Table 1
Contact with Dalits

YES	NO	TOTAL
81	19	100

Table 2
The Kind of Contact

Variables	As farm labourers	Borrowers	As Creditors	Seek certain help	All	Total
No. of respondents	46	17	11	25	1	100

We find as shown in Table 2, there is both labour contact and financial transactions between the Dalits and others.

Table 3
Receive water and food from the hands of Dalits

YES	NO	TOTAL
49	51	100

This is a very sensitive and crucial area in terms of relationship of higher castes with the Dalits. It is really encouraging to find that nearly 50% of the higher caste respondents have no qualms in receiving water and food from the hands of the Dalits. But you could still find the rigidity among half of the higher caste respondents not accepting food and water from the Dalits. 'Yes' indication does not tell that these higher caste groups have commensal relations, their taking food and water at the homes of Dalits.

Table 4
Admission allowed

Variables	Up to the Entrance	Into the house	Into the Kitchen	All	No	Total
No. of respondents	39	39	2	1	19	100

We could see as shown in the table differential kind of treatment meted out to the Dalits by the higher caste groups. For centuries and decades together when the institution of untouchability was in practice, the Dalits can never dream of entering the houses, inner parts of the house of higher caste groups. It is interesting to note a substantial degree of relaxation and allowance meted out to the Dalits by some higher caste groups. However, the rigidity of social distance and physical distance persist in the case of 19 respondents. In other words the kind of relationship varies amongst different caste groups within the so called higher ethnic groups.

Table 5
Taking food along with Dalits

YES	NO	TOTAL
34	66	100

It is interesting to note that both rigidity and relaxation persist among the higher caste groups. As we see in the table, majority of the respondents do not take food along with the Dalits. At the same time, it is encouraging to find 1/3rd of the respondents have no reservation in taking food along with the Dalits. It is really appreciable and remarkable change.

Table 6

Having entered the houses of 'Mala' and 'Madiga':

YES	NO	TOTAL
45	55	100

In this respect also we find reservation and relaxation on the part of the respondents in entering the residences of the Dalits. As we could see from the table more than 50% of respondents are reluctant to enter the houses of Dalits.

Table 7

Any objection in eating at Mala and Madiga homes:

YES	NO	TOTAL
40	60	100

A word of explanation here is necessary because receiving food and water from the hands of Dalits is different from eating in their homes. A Dalit may be a server in a hotel and a customer even though he recognises the server, as a Dalit he may receive water and food from his hand. But going into the homes of Dalits and eating in their homes is different. As the responses indicate the taboo still persists and the traditional value system is such and strong that we find majority of higher caste groups can never think of eating at the homes of the Dalits. A long way to go where you will have free mutual commensal relations between the Dalits and higher caste groups.

We could see considerable growth and development among the Dalits in the field of literacy and standard of living. Ofcourse this is to be attributed to their own efforts and considerable aid extended by the Government in terms of monetary support and encouragement. With the increase in the literacy level and availing themselves of reservation of jobs in Government Departments, a considerable number of Dalits have moved into new jobs from the traditional farm labour and in the case of 'Madiga' community their leather related occupation.

Table 8
The kind of development among the Dalits as seen by the respondents:

Variables	Economic Growth	Literacy level	Social contact	Employment outside the traditional occupation	Total
No. of respondents	29	38	16	17	100

The kind of changes as seen by higher caste groups among 'Mala' and 'Madiga'

In respect to the kind of changes the respondents find in the present study among 'Mala' and 'Madiga' are visible and significant change is their income level has increased as a result of improvement in agriculture and their education and reservations in their case and helping them to move forward considerably in respect of their living standards. We also find a small number with some savings.

Table 9
How disturbed are the higher castes in the growth and development of Dalits

YES	NO	TOTAL
30	70	100

It is a psychological factor when a downtrodden so called lower castes in this respect the Dalits come up, move forward in the economic field and professional field, the higher castes feel disturbed and unhappy. This is what is happening all over India. As we see at present a great movement, agitation going on in the country for and against certain percentage of reservation in respect of OBCs. Of course there is unquestionable reservation in the case of Dalits. As we could see here, in the present instance majority of the respondents find the onward growth of Dalits disturbing them.

MEASURES TAKEN BY THE GOVERNMENT TO IMPROVE DALITS

As indicated by the respondents within their knowledge, the Government both union and State taking measures to help the Dalits in respect to housing, education, employment and general welfare of the Dalits.

Table 10
Respondents' assessment of the ameliorative measures initiated by the Government in respect to Dalits:

Variables	Good	Satisfied	Not satisfied	No response	Total
No. of respondents	22	16	8	54	100

As we could see from the table, many of the respondents have no idea and or not capable of providing details in respect of this question.

Table 11
The kind of relationship with Dalits

Variables	Intimate	As equals	Quite friendly	Business like	Keep distance	Total
No. of respondents	18	33	38	08	16	100

We see differential kind of intimacy and distance maintained by the higher castes with the Dalits. The figures in the table may be taken as representative situation all over India. This kind of closeness and distance will persist for several decades to come. It is not forecasting that the Dalits and higher caste groups mixing will lead even upto the point of marital relations.

The respondents were asked the way in which the higher caste groups are helping the Dalits. The responses indicate a small number of respondents lend money to the Dalits, help them in the field of education and involve them in social activities. But the majority of the respondents do not render any service to the Dalits in their geographical area.

Of the 100 respondents 6 are affiliated to congress and the rest have no affiliation with any political party.

In the foregoing analysis though restricted to 100 respondents in A.P. and Tamil Nadu the responses in general reflect the ongoing situation all over India in regard to the Dalits and the kind of nexus of relationship that exists between the higher caste groups and the Dalits. The process is a socio-cultural movement bringing about changes through legislation, realization and enlightenment on both sides.

FIELD DATA RELATED TO MALA AND MADIGA COMMUNITY

The Scheduled Castes or Dalits number around 800 all over India. In another chapter in the book details are provided in respect of the major sub-groups among the Dalits. Mala and Madiga are the two distinct Dalit groups in South India with differing names in Tamil and Kannada. (for the sake of clarity especially in South India Mala and Madiga caste names are used referring to them) Pariaher is the name in Tamil for Mala and chakkiliar is the name for 'Madiga' and Madhari is also used for 'Madiga'. Though the conditions of Mala all over India with different nomenclatures, their level of living predominantly is same except during recent decades with educational qualifications, reservation of posts in Government departments. A small percentage of men and women have risen to high and very high levels in economic terms as well as in the political field. As an illustration of the situation we have selected at random 100 respondents of Dalits, 50 from the Kanyakumari district in Tamil Nadu and 50 from the district Chittoor in A.P.

In most parts of the country Dalits' residential areas are at a distance and isolated form the residential area of higher caste groups. They were not only socially distanced but geographically also.

Table 12
Respondents' settlements from the higher caste settlements

YES	NO	TOTAL
69	31	100

One could see majority mala settlements are isolated from the higher castes settlements. Further, it is interesting to note 31 respondents have indicated, that their settlements are close to or of continuation of higher caste settlements. In casc of isolated settlements of Mala the distance ranges from half to 1 kilometre.

Table 13
Owning a house

YES	NO	TOTAL
70	30	100

One of the basic requirements of minimal level of life of a family is owning a house whatever may be the type. One could imagine that 30 families in the sample do not own a house. One could imagine their flight without a house of their own.

The study also tried to look into the type of houses owned by 70 respondents. We choose three types of houses and the details are shown in the following table.

Table 14
Type of houses owning

Variables	Pucca	Semi Pucca	Katcha	Total
No. of respondents	36	10	24	70

These houses were built during the past 20 years at various periods.

It was an accepted norm of physical distance of residence especially in rural areas. But in urban centres, it is difficult to enforce the principal of isolation of residences in the case of the Dalits.

Table 15
Distance

½ K.M.	1 K.M.	1 ½ K.M.	2 K.M.	3 K.M.	No distance	Total
35	37	7	6	1	14	100

One could see varying physical distance between the Madiga settlements and other higher caste groups.

Table 16
House owning

YES	NO	TOTAL
62	38	100

In respect to owning a house whatever may be the type we find 38 respondent families don't own houses. May be they share with others or of course live in rented houses. As we have mentioned in the case of Mala we find similar situation in regard to Madiga. This situation not owning of houses is true of a considerable number of Mala and Madiga families. They don't have the basic minimal requirement – a house of their own.

In the case of those who own houses the type of houses varies.

Pukka houses	30
Semi pukka	12
Kutcha	8
Old thatched houses	12

We see the respondent families residing in different type of houses. In view of their level of living owning a house whatever may be the type and plinth area is a luxury in their case. These houses were built during the past 18 years. Some houses are built before 5 years and others are built during various periods.

In respect to the respondents who don't have houses of their own some live in rented houses and others share with their relatives.

A question was asked to the respondents whether their wives are literate, 43 respondents said 'yes' and the rest of them said 'No'. It may be mentioned here of late, percentage of literate women among the Dalits in general and here in the case of Madiga it is on increase. Of the literate women 50% are employed in somc kind of job. Thc family size of the sampled ranges from 3 to 7.

Majority of the respondents are engaged in farming and a small number are doing some business and some are employed. When it comes to the monthly income in the case of the respondents it ranges from Rs.500 to 20000. The higher income mentioned here is in respect to Madiga members employed in S.V. University, Tirupati. In a sense, some of these people are at apex level and enjoy higher standard of life.

It is interesting to find 37 respondents are employed in Government organisations. Some of the professionals are engaged in drumbeating on festive occasions, marriages and funerals. This has been their age long profession and it survives still.

Table 17

Kind of assistance received from the Government

House site	A grant for house building	Allocation of Land	Assistance for children's education	Loan	Financial assistance for self-employment
30	33	17	7	31	10

We see here substantial help has been received for several purposes. It is really appreciable that they have applied and got the assistance.

Table 18
Entry allowed to higher caste houses

Upto the portico	Inside the house	Kitchen
45	40	15

It is interesting to note that considerable relaxation has taken place between the Madiga respondents and higher caste groups in respect to physical admission to some parts of the house. For several centuries and even for a few recent decades there was no question of Madiga or other Dalits being allowed into the house and that too into the kitchen. It is really appreciable to see 15 respondents have allowance to enter the kitchen which may be considered something like a sanctorum in the house.

Table 19
Higher castes receiving drink/water and food from Madiga Community

Yes	No	Total
40	60	100

In this respect also as shown in the table relaxation and rigidity is operating today. This kind of higher caste people receiving water, drink or food from the hands of the Dalits a few years ago is inconceivable.

Table 20
Practicing of Untouchability

Yes	No	Total
63	37	100

Even though untouchability was constitutionally abolished in India, abolition of untouchability does not bring in immediate results in practice. It is a question of traditional value system and deep rooted attitudes which operate especially in rural areas, expecting immediate change in the observation of untouchability is a complex and difficult factor. It depends on the individual will to be or not be. One can write at length on this horrible practice of untouchability.

Even though slavery is an institution which existed in the United States until 1881, there was no question of untouchability between the whites and blacks. But when we look at India the untouchability question was a serious and an inhuman one.

In the rural areas, almost everybody knows including the children as to who is who and what to caste he belongs. Practicising untouchability by the higher caste groups was taken by them as honour and superior status. The higher caste man may be poor compared to a Dalit in economic terms and educational or professional attainment, but this higher casteman feels superior to the Dalit. Caste is inherited and acquired. May be a long way to go for the practice of untouchability becoming an age old practice and will remain as a historical custom.

Table 21
The degree of interaction between the higher caste people to the Madigas

Very closely	Somewhat closely	Not at all closely	Depending on purpose	Total
10	56	11	23	100

Here also we look at the kind of activities and functions where in we find meeting and interactions on the part of the higher caste groups and Madigas. These occasions were normally marriage functions, celebration of some deities and in work places and so on.

Table 22
Treated as equal

Yes	No	Total
39	61	100

Here also we find social distance persisting in between the Dalits and the higher caste groups. If is found in the study, the higher caste people seldom invite the Madiga to their family functions, rituals and celebrations. It is also found in some cases the higher caste groups do not allow the Madiga enter shrines and temples. Further, as it has been an age long practice on the part of the higher caste groups not allowing the Dalits to draw water from the wells used by them, though in many areas this isolation and rigidity is slowly disappearing.

One may describe and narrate practices observed by the Dalits and expected by the higher caste groups. Here we may cite as reported by some respondents that the Dalits are taboo in wearing the slippers in the presence of higher caste, not hold umbrella and keep standing while higher caste people sitting and they were expected to fold their hands and dhoti should be only upto their knees, the towel should not hang on the shoulder and should be in the armpit. Today, as reported by the respondents some of these practices are disappearing. As pointed out in the introductory part change is taking place on both sides.

Table 23
Still following the traditional practices

Drum-beating	Burial and cremation of the dead	Thoti	Skinning and burial of dead cattle	Making Slippers	All activities	Total
8	14	14	8	14	42	100

We find that to a large extent the Madiga communities still follow in a sense the above mentioned jajmani functions.

Since the Madiga are mostly poor and many below poverty line depend for their farming purposes, housing, food, marriages etc. borrow money from professional moneylenders, farmers and sometimes apply for loans. The responses indicate that the majority of them go in for some kind of loan.

We also find a small number of Madiga respondents lending money to higher caste people.

Table 24
The extent to which the community avails itself the beneficiary schemes introduced by the Government

To a large extent	To some extent	Very rarely	Not at all	Total
5	33	45	17	100

Some NGOs operate among the Madiga for their improvement.

As we have seen, the Madiga as well as other Dalit groups and the hierarchy of the higher caste are slowly changing. The changes taking place on both sides are encouraging, but a long way to go to attain social equality.

It may be mentioned here in general, the overall or normal living conditions of the entire ethnic communities which go with different local, lingual nomenclatures all over India is given of late a generic name Dalits. As in the case of Mala, we have chosen a sample Madiga (Madari, Chamar, Chakkiliar etc.) from the districts of Kanyakumari and Chittoor. As mentioned above, we find largely uniform levels of life among the Madiga and we have chosen just 50 families from each district of Madiga community. Before we go into the analysis of the data obtained, we may briefly describe the traditional type of Madiga community.

Earlier they were also treated as untouchables. Traditionally, especially in South India they were engaged in making leather buckets used for lift irrigation. Madiga families were attached to certain families, which was fixed. This relationship was considered legal right on the part of the Madiga families serving their clients, farming families. In return to this service they were paid in kind (grain at the time of harvest). Besides, their making and mending leather buckets earlier they were also making chappals out of leather to the families they serve. Of late, on the advent of electric motors and pumpsets and massive production and sale of different varieties of chappals, shoes etc. not only the Madiga lost their occupation in leather bucket making but making chappals also. Along with their traditional occupation they were mostly engaged in farm labour – both men and women.

As mentioned above they go by different names but their status and the way they were and even now treated something very low. Even though the Malas and Madigas socially enjoy the same treatment and social distance, they have been extremely exclusive communities. The amazing thing is, these two communities don't have commensal relations. Each community claiming and behaving superiority over the other. Though minimal and considerable changes are taking place during the recent decades along the entire line of castes we find not even an iota of change has taken place on the part of the Mala and Madiga. Their views and their attitudes towards each other are fixed and stand rigid.

Now we come down to the analysis of the small sample.

Table 25
Madiga settlement whether isolated from the higher caste

Yes	No	Total
75	25	100

Before we move on to the figures related to settlement of the Madiga may be centuries over predominantly the residential parts of the Dalits including the Madiga were isolated ones from the settlements of the higher caste groups. In the present study we find 75% of Madiga settlements are isolated ones or away from the residential parts of higher caste groups. For decades we could see how the respondent families are economically occupied.

We find that some of the families of the respondents appear to be relatively better off compared to the conditions a couple of decades ago.

Table 26
Occupation of the respondents

Variables	Farming	Small business	Labour	Employee	Unemployed	Total
No. of respondents	41	4	24	1	30	100

Table 27
The range of monthly income

Variables	Below Rs.1000	1000-2000	2001-3000	3001-4000	Above 4000	Total
No. of respondents	43	25	13	15	4	100

Number of respondents or any family member in Government Service

In regard to the employment either in Government or Private Sector, 39 respondents or family members are employed in Government or Private Sectors.

We find a large number of respondents have received some kind of assistance from the Government. Only small numbers have indicated that they have not received any assistance. May be they did not seek any assistance from the Government.

We find the value system and the customs in practice and customs in practice differ as we could see the variegated accessibility of the Madiga respondents to the residential partners of the higher caste people.

Similar to the above aspect of accessibility, the respondents were asked whether the higher caste people receive water, coffee, tea or food from the hands of the 'Madiga' community, 52 respondents have said that the higher caste people receive from their hands the items mentioned above and the others indicated below 'No'.

Table 28

Types of Assistance received from the Government

Variables	House Site	Grant for Building house	Allocation of Land	Assistance for children's education	Financial Assistance for Self-Employment	Loan	Not received any assistance	Total
No. of respondents	43	19	6	6	14	3	9	100

Table 29

Respondents' accessibility to the houses of higher caste groups

Upto the Portico	Inside the house	To the Kitchen	Not allowed	Total
37	41	12	10	100

Table 30

The closeness of interacting between the higher caste people and the respondents

Variables	Very closely	Some what closely	Not at all closely	Closely depending upon the purpose	No response	Total
No. of respondents	12	29	22	33	4	100

In respect to the festivals, religious rituals, social functions like marriages, the Madiga community mixes and interacts with the higher caste groups in different degrees. It may be mentioned here that during elections to the local bodies, legislature etc. often the higher caste people go close to the Dalits and solicit their help and their votes. This is one area wherein the Dalits are gaining strength and their number is recognised and it enhances their importance facilitating their free movement and importance accorded to their voice and opinion.

It may also be noted as indicated by the respondents that there is considerable change on the part of the higher caste groups in calling and addressing Dalit men and women. Earlier, the higher caste people even in the case of young they always used singular in the local language while addressing the Dalits even if they were middle aged and old. Now there is a gradual change in the manner of addressing, behaviour on the part of the higher caste groups vis-à-vis Dalits.

When it comes to the higher caste groups treating the Dalits equal to them, we find considerable difference.

Only 27 respondents have indicated that they are not treated equal to higher caste groups. One could see the inequality still persisting largely when we look at the social position of the Dalits.

Table 31
Various functions in which the Madiga community traditionally are engaged

Variables	Drum beating	Burial ceremony of dead	Thoti (Messages)	Skinning & burial of dea cattle	Not engaged in any function	Total
No. of respondents	35	32	37	17	9	100

We see though certain changes are taking place among the Madiga community we find the traditional cultural links and sorts of services on the part of the Madiga still continue. These are the services creating inter-dependence between the Dalits and the higher caste groups.

Overall, as per the respondents we find considerable awakening on the part of the Dalits under study and gradual increase of confidence and their importance and a degree of determination and boldness to seek help from government organisations. On the other hand, there is a considerable mellowing down on the part of several higher caste groups.

CHAPTER 5

Case Studies

SREERAMULAVARIPALLE, VEMANNA, AGED ABOUT 62 YEARS

1. **[The author has visited a few Dalit villages and interacted with some individuals who are in a sense elderly leaders of the Dalit Communities. We now look into the details given by one Vemanna 62 Year Old Dalit. (Mala)]**

The following details were given by Vemanna.

This village called Sreeramulavaripalle was provided by the state government in 1972. The village settlement area comprises 1 acre 10 cents. The Government has helped each family in terms of building material worth around Rs.7500/-. Nobody in the village owns any land except the house site for which patta was given by the government. Almost all the able bodied people both men and women work in the Rishi Valley farm area. Rishi Valley is the only institution which economically sustains some of the families in return to our labour contribution.

During the past decades, we have suffered a great deal in terms of food and with great difficulty, we brought up our children. I may just mention here during my youth the wage for one day labour was only 4 Annas (The old denomination before the advent of decimal system). In those days with an amount of Rs.10/-, we were able to buy enough of vegetables and food grains and lead comparatively a happy life. But today even if you take Rs.100/-, it is insufficient.

To begin with, there were only 8 Families in 1963. All of us as mentioned above were engaged in sweeping and farm labour at the Rishi Valley Estate.

I may mention something about myself. In my youth until I reached my 50 plus, I was a heavy boozer. As a result of this excessive drinking I fell ill, and was taken to a few hospitals and ultimately I got better at Sathya Sai Hospital in Puttaparthi. Now I refrain from alcohol. But I am addicted to smoking of beedies and I am unable to refrain from smoking. I am blessed with two sons and a daughter and the two sons hire themselves as painters and through their earnings the family is supported in meeting the minimum requirements of our existence. My wife works at the Rishi Valley on daily wages. In a sense, Rishi Valley is the caretaker of our village helping us when we fall ill. They have helped us with the supply of cows and sheep. And during recent years with this kind of help the youth in the community is slowly progressive. The contribution from the government was only the street roads apart from that there was nothing in terms of loan or any financial assistance extended to the families in the village. The Management of the Rishi Valley earlier was concerned with our welfare but today the people in the Management are different, they have become very strict, they do not show the kind of attention which we enjoyed earlier. Though the road was laid by the Government, what is required is the drainage, as of today there is no drainage. Since we are all landless we can not apply for any loan from any financial institution for buying cows and sheep, since the bankers and cooperative societies insist on security of land. We suffer from this limitation. No way to borrow money to improve ourselves. There are a few children who have passed school final but they are not able to secure any advertised job in government and private organisations since they can not afford to bribe the prospective employers. Even in the case of reserved posts, one has to bribe the authority. No way to get any job even though the candidate fulfills all the requirements as stipulated in the advertisement. He doesn't get the job because he has no money to bribe the middle men of the employer. It is the first time that I sat on a chair. Seldom, we sat on chair, when the higher caste people are present. Traditionally we use to stand in the presence of the higher caste people in the community. We never use to sit at the same level with them.

In respect to our interaction with the 'MADIGA' Community, it is restricted. We keep a clear-cut boundary between ourselves and the Madiga. It has been there from the beginning. Though, both the communities are referred to as 'Dalits', we consider the 'Madigas' inferior to us. The reason, as we understand is their flaying of Caracas of cattle and eating the dead animals and they process cattle hides. Though we are moving a bit closer to the caste Hindus slowly we maintain the same critical distance from the Madiga right from the beginning. Absolutely no change in our relations with them, since we feel we are superior to the Madigas.

Since in a major way, we are supported by the Rishi Valley, I may briefly mention, the system that is followed by that institution. Primarily it is an educational institution but they follow a discriminatory and divisive way of imparting to the children. The major institution comprises children from the highly influenced and rich families. But whereas, in the case of children of low income families they run a separate school. Since our children are the poor they had to join this school. I understand that the curriculum and the facilities at this school are at inferior level and instead of teaching the children the system that is followed in other schools which are of standard type is denied and the children in this lower type of school, majority of them do not go beyond X class. Especially, our children are admitted to this lower level of school. After their IX and X class these children are employed as sweepers or engaged in menial jobs. In a way, it is a boundary for us all the time lingering and working at lower levels. I came to know that sub-standards of instruction are used at the lower school which is meant for low income groups. Usually, the children admitted at the school are older compared to the other children. By the time our children, some of them who complete their VIII & X standards will be 18 to 20 years in age. That is a disadvantage for these children to apply for some jobs. And so, as mentioned above these children are employed by the Rishi Valley as sweepers and put into some lower standard jobs. We have to accept this situation since there are no other means to us. The one that I am referring to is named as rural education centre. But the pitiful thing is not even a single child who has studied in this centre has obtained a degree or secured a job in Government. This is the record of this Rural Education Centre (REC). It is a composite village but Harijans are part of it because it was established by Rishi Valley. Normally the settlement of Dalits (Mala or Madiga) are physically far from the Caste Hindu settlement. It appears from the beginning it was not only social cultural distance, but physical too.

2. [The following are the ideas and impressions expressed by one Sri Narayana Swamy, Teacher, Madanapalle on Dalits and their progress in the rural areas and neighbourhood known to him].

The first thing I would like to point out is, there is no exercising power and authority on either side in respect of Caste Hindus and Dalits. So far as I have observed, the Dalits have no great expectations and forward thinking in terms of improving their way of life. The higher caste groups also are not bothered and rarely extend any economic or financial help to the Dalits. Since, the Dalits do not have ideas and plans to move forward economically they seldom seek support from the higher caste groups. As I mentioned above the higher caste groups also in general are not interested and bothered about development on the part of the Dalits. In the case of the Dalit children who have passed school final and PUC do not plan for further academic growth and employment, but try to imitate in dressing, in traveling on buses, two wheelers and cars similar to the better off rich people. Their attention is more on their appearance not in terms of trying for a job, earn some money and improve their family conditions. Often, I find among the youngsters in the Dalit communities an attempt to be different from the old people and distancing themselves from traditions of Dalit cultural activities.

I would like to make some observations that the Government is trying to ameliorate the living conditions of the Dalits and in this regard the teachers posted to schools where Dalit children are also enrolled are expected to pay special attention to the Dalit children, but they feel discouraged because Dalit children are not effectively responding and studying up to the expectations of the teacher. This is a discouraging factor for the teachers, vis-à-vis the Dalit children.

The financial assistance provided to the higher caste people is utilized properly for productive and development purposes, whereas in the case of Dalits mostly they misutilise the assistance towards consumer goods and not spending the money for which it was given. Another interesting factor that I have noticed is the teachers posted to the schools in Dalit colonies are reluctant to join the schools and even if they join they feel unhappy because the Dalit parents do not send their children on time regularly to their classes. This thin and poor attendance is a discouraging factor to the teachers. Some of the teachers shared with me this kind of feeling. Here, the question is lack of value and importance attached to education by the Dalit parents.

3. Redeppa Reddy, a farmer and a political leader

I find a major change among the higher caste groups in their interaction and working relationships with the Dalits. The Caste Hindu farmers are trying to be very careful in addressing, communicating and interacting with the Dalits. While they go for seeking the Dalit labour, they address them by calling full name sometimes using plural in addressing them. Earlier may be for centuries or decades the mode was different. Usually, the higher caste people, well to do or poor use to address the elderly Dalits also in singular not in plural. This is the slight change I find among higher caste groups. Here, as we know the Dalits had to address the higher caste groups with due respect usually in plural form.

In this context though not during the period of my grand father and father, the Brahmin Priest and local Brahmin leaders when they were to write names of people belonging to 'Reddy' and 'Naidu' communities never used to write after the name the suffix of the community (Reddy, Naidu) but invariably they used their suffix "Aiyar" "Ayyangar" 'Sharma' depending on the distinctive sects.

In respect to the financial assistance provided to the Dalits the total amount for an individual family does not reach in toto but on the way at several points leakage takes place. Unfortunately, officials and local political leaders swallow a larger part of the amount sanctioned and meant for the individual Dalit. With the increase in the number of Dalits to whom financial assistance is provided eaually the number of exploiters also increased.

When some amount is sanctioned to the Dalits, only a few people will be there to explain and guide the loanees or the clients, the way in which the sanctioned amount is to be utilized. Besides, the local politicians and the officials along the conduit of delivery of assistance squeeze a larger part of the amount meant to reach the applicant. This is not new. This kind of pilferage and bribing is known to the administration. I wonder whether a day would come when the whole sanctioned amount reaches the applicant. I have seen the villages in which this kind of pilferage is increasing day-by-day. The culprits are the politicians and the administrative personnel. As of now, there is no watchdog for this kind of shameful phenomenon.

Though, the policy is to alleviate poverty it is not taking place as it should be. Obviously, awareness is to be created among the people so that they know their rights, privileges from the Government or any other organization. If this awareness and sensitivity is created among the poor, may be in a matter of 10 to 15 years we may reduce number of families who struggle below poverty line.

4. Thettu Harijanavada

[It is a constituent hamlet of Thettu village and Panchayat. It comprises 160 families and they belong to Madiga community (cobblers). As per the version of the people it is over a century old. To begin with, there were only 18 families engaged in traditional occupation of making and mending leather buckets used in lift irrigation and also engaged in making slippers out of leather. In the following pages we have an account in first person narrated by one Eswarappa and Avulappa. Both are around 65 years of age].

We have not received any assistance from the Government so far. During those olden days we were able to sustain ourselves through the wages we earned. Today, with the daily wage say Rs.50/- hardly we can buy sufficient rice and other vegetables to sustain per day. Almost all the 160 families in the village are poor and we should say that they are below the poverty line. Almost all the people male and female are engaged in farm labour. Of the 160 families 40 families don't have their own houses but they have house sites. For a long time now houseless people have been trying to get some assistance from the Government towards their modest and simple houses. But so far assistance has not reached them. But when the concerned officials are contacted they give vague answers and assure that the money will be provided to these people in a short time. These verbal promises and assurances are continuing indefinitely.

Till today January 2006, none of the 160 families here has received any loan for purchasing cows or buffaloes as a source of supplementing income through sale of milk though they have provided housing with financial assistance. The authorities have not taken into account size of the family. For instance, there is one family in this village where there are more than 10 children and that family too received the same amount for a similar kind of unit. We feel, the authorities should consider the size of the family too and atleast helping the family for two houses. Of the 160 families in this village 60 of them do not possess any land. The main stay for them is farm labour.

To a question whether there are graduates in the village, the group mentioned there are a few and respond to advertisements indicating availability of jobs and that too sometimes specifically mentioning the jobs reserved for Dalits. The graduates and also those who have completed secondary school apply for the jobs even though, some of them get selected in the interviews do not get the jobs since the families lack money to bribe the employers and some intermediary agents. That has been the fate for the few educated youth in the village.

The paradoxical situation is, it is the 'Malas' who secured jobs and relatively they are better off compared to our 'Madiga' community. As mentioned earlier even with requisite qualification, our youth do not get jobs in the Government because we do not have money often ranging from 10 to 20 thousand to bribe the people. We feel very much for this for our educated youth, the problem is we don't have money and we cannot obtain any loan. That is the stalemate. Even though jobs are advertised in the newspapers the educated youth look into the advertisements and do not prepare for competitive examinations feeling they cannot afford money to bribe the people even-though, they get selected for the post. To get any certificate or a paper from a local revenue or development office, we have to visit the office atleast seven times. The officials there do not respond, give evasive answers and lame excuses. That has been our plight. The officials exploit our weakness and poverty.

Because of this discouraging experience, of late we have given up hopes and any attempt to apply for any help from the Government. The way the Government officials treat us is simply de-motivating us to initiate any attempt for our development.

We may cite here a very highly intelligent action on the part of the higher caste groups. Some of them with some assurance and protection borrowed our certificates replace the caste names with Madiga as their community and got the jobs. Unfortunately we have become gullible loosers by this kind of cheating and exploitation. We don't have the strength to fight with them.

We were told that Krishna Madiga is our leader fighting for our development. We think that he is serious, genuine and organizes meetings, encourages our community but unfortunately the organizers and local leaders of our community exploit the situation. Supposing Krishna Madiga has mobilized and secured certain amount of money for a specific village of our community, his followers swindle away the money and very little reaches the intended beneficiaries. To a question whether the caste Hindu farmers extend any help to the Madiga community they said they exploit them wherever there is a chance and try to purchase lands belonging to the Dalits at low price. The owner of the fair price shop here cheats us in different ways. In case, when we don't have money to purchase rice and kerosene within 3 days of the announcement, he sells away the commodities in black market. When we question him about the quota that we get, he will tell us that you have failed to purchase within 3 days from the date of announcement, so you have lost what was due to you. We are helpless in this regard. The better higher caste groups in the neighbourhood are least concerned about our plight.

As a consequence, the well-to-do higher caste groups ill treating and discriminating the Dalits, a considerable number of youth in Dalit communities are joining the Naxalite group. The youth in the local villages are not in a position to revolt against higher caste groups, ill treating the Dalits. This could be seen predominantly in the state of A.P, Orissa and Bihar.

CHAPTER 6

Caste Dynamics Influencing Development

Of several affinities that foster unity, bonds of enduring relationship, solidarity and concerted social action on the part of the people such as territorial, regional, racial, ethnic, political, ideological, religious, sectarian, lingual, occupational and professional, the social institution of caste is a strong and enduring one. The institution of caste is unique in India. It is an unchanging ascribed status and identity for an individual. One may change his political and ideological views and change his religious faith and move from one region to another, but one's caste identity does not change. Caste is both a unifying and divisive force. The forces of caste for and against are apparent in every field. One could witness the caste dynamics operating in the villages creating enmity, cliques, factions, and rivalries, one caste group fighting against another. Caste generates competition, both subtle and vibrant with expression of emotions. Competition by itself is not negative. It promotes improvement and advancement. A healthy competition is a welcome factor in order to make the caste groups in the villages compete with one another and excel and improve their lives.

When it comes to helping people caste promotes favouritism helping the group that belongs to the political leaders and administrators although we have all the rules, regulations and specifications as to whom the help should reach yet caste factors influence the delivery of goods and services to the deserving minority caste groups.

It is well-nigh impossible to eliminate the negative and detrimental caste born attitudes from some caste groups. The problem with caste system is its rigidity in attitude. Caste discriminations are more visible and active in rural areas. One may come across instances wherein numerically dominant and politically influential caste groups are barriers in assistance reaching the lower caste groups or downtrodden ones. One may speak at length about the dynamics and the historical tradition and hereditarily inherited patterns of behaviour associated with different caste groups. As we discuss below there are positive and negative elements in the institution.

In the context of rural development with multiple development and welfare programmes, the development workers at the field level should have some understanding of the caste dynamics. They have to keep in mind the forces that are in operation and manoeuvre over these forces to see that help reaches the deserving and they should also work as effective social change agents to bring about harmony in the rural communities to work towards development of the entire community.

Here, we may mention that it is not only the field workers who are to be sensitive to these forces but the entire administration in the field of rural development should be sensitive and wise-enough to operate in such a way that over a period of time we succeed and gradually reduce the prejudices and stereotypes attributed to different caste groups. In this context, a brief understanding of the emergence operation and slowly declining caste system in India is relevant and interesting.

It is much easier to say what caste is not than what caste is. It is not class, for it consists of rich and poor, literate and illiterate and of high and low mental caliber. It is not colour. An upper-caste man may be black and a Harijan quite fair in complexion. It is not Aryan and non-Aryan, conqueror and conquered. It is not even occupation. Many occupations, mostly of artisans, overwhelmingly identify themselves with particular castes, but the main occupation, agriculture is open to all. Hundreds of castes and sub-castes live on the plough.

So occupation alone has not caused caste. Occupational distribution is not now based on caste.

Caste is not exclusively Hindu or exclusively Indian. It obtains elsewhere too in a modified form. Nor does the present caste structure bear much relation to the traditional four *varnas*.

Each caste embodies in itself its rites, taboos, do's and don'ts in food, drinking and matrimony.

Whatever sets off a group in any way may be sufficient to make it a caste in India. If groups diverge within an established caste they become recognized as sub-castes, perhaps finally to develop into wholly separate castes. Caste is a way of thought that the Hindu has tried to universalize.

CASTES ARE ENDOGAMOUS

All Indian castes are in theory strictly endogamous; intermarriage is intolerable. All possess an intrinsic, unchangeable worth. Thus they automatically rank themselves. Caste embraces one's life activities in their entirety from cradle to grave. Each possesses an occupation, a mode of life and customs, a set of prescribed rituals, inherently peculiar to it. The greater the restriction and prohibition incumbent upon it, the less it relaxes to comfort and indifference, the more spiritual it is, the higher its grade. In consequence it is also more pollutable, and so its restrictions are drawn closer. The wider the gap with the lower classes, the greater becomes its purity.

Life cannot be lived in parts or compartments; it is an integrated whole. So, religion, man's spiritual food, is fused with caste or the other way about.

The *Rig Veda*, the most ancient and sacred of Hindu hymns, does not talk of the caste system. Caste existed during the epic period. Caste is a hierarchy and has no bearing to the original four *varnas* in its content and functions. Hundreds of castes are sub-divided into sub-castes and sub-castes run into thousands. Among Brahmins alone there are over two thousand sub-castes and even among the so-called untouchables, over five hundred. It is the sub-castes which give Hindu society its character. Each caste embodies in itself its rites, taboos, do's and don'ts in food, drink and matrimony.

Caste not only governs one's manner of life, it also fixes the place in society in which one lives. Caste structure, to a larger extent, conditions human relationships and sentiments. "Caste gives its directions for recognition, acceptance, consecration, and sacramental dedication, and *vice versa*, of a human being on his appearance in this world. It has for infancy, pupilage, and manhood, its ordained methods of sucking, sipping, drinking, eating, and voiding; of washing, rinsing, anointing, and smearing; of clothing, dressing and ornamenting; of sitting, rising and reclining; of moving, visiting and traveling; of speaking, reading, listening, and reciting; and of meditating, singing, working, playing, and fighting. It has its laws for social and religious rights, privileges, and occupations; for instructing, training and educating; for obligation, duty, and ceremony; for errors, sins and transgressions; for intercommunication, avoidance, and excommunication; for defilement, ablution, and purification; for fines, chastisements, imprisonments, mutilations, banishments, and capital executions. It deals with death, burial and burning; and with commemoration, assistance, and injury after death. It interferes, in short, with all the relations, and events of life and with what precedes and follows...life".

This winding has been going on for centuries and to unwind the whole thing in a span of few decades would take time.

Caste hierarchy was built on inter-caste relationships. It was the elaborate proliferation of the rules governing inter-caste relationships and the meticulous enforcement of them that guaranteed the separateness and integrity of each caste. It was this complete separation of the various social strata which made India's class structure unique.

Caste grew with the sanction of the society. Conditions such as geographical isolation, static society, foreign aggression, rural social structure, influence of the religion, differences of races, and lack of education, have favoured the continued existence of the caste system. However arbitrary it is, it was spontaneous in the growth. It has played a positive cementing role. It has been a unifying force. In the long chequered history of India, it has held together the fabric of Indian society. Caste in unison with Hinduism resisted the onslaught of successive foreign invasions and centuries of alien rule and preserved the content of Hindu culture.

Caste reveals itself most obviously and most rigidly in everyday life, through the concept of pollution, a concept fundamental to the Hindu way of life. Caste which begins with pollution develops into a way of life. The concept of pollution is simply maddening, carried to meaningless, illogical and incomprehensible extremities. How fantastic are its magnitude and ramifications! There is pollution by sight, pollution by approach, pollution by touch, pollution by drink, pollution by food, pollution by matrimony, pollution by travel over sea and so on. The faith or the belief works in this way; God has ordained everything and caste too is His making and so preserve and live the tenets, rituals, taboos and everything that go with each caste.

Caste functions in a multitude of ways, diet regulations for every occasion; ritual bathing, caste deities, the manner of worship, fasts, the colour of one's clothes, the colour of the flowers one wears, the shape of one's ornaments, the pattern of one's rituals, decoration, ancestral worship etc. Further we have the Indian village structure and during festive and ceremonious occasions the distribution of work or division of labour is assigned to each sub-caste and each attends to a specific item of work arranged in gradation underlying prestige and privilege.

CHANGES DESPITE RIGIDITY

Despite the rigidity, conservatism and complexity of caste, changes have been taking place in the system. Many forces opposed the evils of caste system, Jainism, Buddhism, Lingayatism, Sikhism, Christianity and the movements of Arya Samaj and Brahma Samaj and social reformers have proclaimed their opposition to caste. Modern education with its democratic ideals and values, industrialization and urbanization, money power, various movements of social emancipation, increase in the means of communication, political awakening, the emergence of legal machinery, appearance of new social classes and most important the universal adult franchise have tended to weaken the caste system.

Opposition to the caste system works in two ways. People do not believe in either predestined superiority or predestined inferiority. With all these things, the change in the villages is obviously very slow. Caste breathes quite healthily even today in the rural areas.

But, on the other hand, by the very nature and composition of the social structure in towns and cities, caste is ineffective; it does not raise its head, does not make much ado and is fast sinking. Here, no segregation, no discrimination in buses, trains, restaurants and other public places is possible. It is dying a slow and a natural death.

The villager's contact with the town slowly undermines the hold of caste on his thought. As a result of modern education and industrialization, the sanctity of caste has begun to be questioned. The caste hierarchy is slowly crumbling down.

The Constitution forbids the practice of untouchability and does not recognize caste. Though law holds itself against caste and untouchability, yet does not operate by itself but in a social environment. Transformation must take place in the attitude and beliefs of people.

The political parties in their own pursuit for power are reviving the disintegrating caste system. The slow dying embers of casteism are kindled by the politicians at every level during the elections.

The process of democracy is changing the old order; the old structure is being restructured, the functions are changing, power is redistributed, and the whole fabric of the socio-economic order is reconditioned, in a manner unthought of and unheard of before.

Caste differences were accepted as cultural and social norms. So long as it was not challenged, it flourished. Had it been challenged in the earlier centuries, it would have crumbled long ago. Many factors made this institution thrive for a pretty long period. This winding has been going on for centuries and to unwind the whole thing in a matter of few decades would demand a basic change in people's attitudes. For caste lies in the mind of man. Let us hope that at least in the years and decades to come it will become a thing of the past and a primitive institution.

[**Source:** E. Desingu Setty, "Caste Hierarchy: The Crumbling Edifice", *Social Welfare*, Vol. XXV, No.9, December 1978, New Delhi.]

CHAPTER 7

Approaches of Dalits Development

The Dalits in India numbering around 800 go by different ethnic names. They constitute roughly $1/7^{th}$ of India's population and they are the majority group in poverty and people below poverty line. The question of Dalits development is a massive one. It is not an individual or a family. The issues or problems are not single, but varied in type depicting their struggle at the bottom level in the caste hierarchy. Caste system and division of functions for centuries have contributed to stagnation, confined to menial labour among the Dalits. They were made to be content with meagre wages paid to them. So long they were sure of farm labour and a kind of patronage by the landed gentry, the higher castes, there was little motivation to strive forward on the part of the Dalits.

Based on intimate and prolonged observation of several Dalit individuals and communities, it is to be pointed out that their aspirations and desires were and are limited to their basic needs. No high aspirations because, they do not see the resources, possibilities, knowledge and skills on their part. Very often they have determined and accepted their fate, level and their way of life. What has been the emancipation of the Dalits over centuries. The movement or the impetus started only after Indian independence and the father of the nation was the progenitor of the movement aiming at the upliftment of the Dalits.

So long you perpetuate injustice, discrimination, differential treatment meted out to the deprived Dalits, you are not civilized and a human being. The role of Karmik

Theory and in its belief which served as a defence and justification for different advantages, deprivations, limitations and special advantages and privileges enjoyed by the higher castes deserves to be taken note of. It is really amazing that over centuries as in the case of slaves in the United States, the discrimination meted out to the Dalits and the way they were treated and their position in the societal hierarchy was accepted as a norm determined by the divine and man has no role in it and he cannot meddle with divinely decided or fate has ordained. This kind of belief or formula was advantageous in various decreasing degrees to the *Varna* – the caste groups in the social hierarchy. So long the poor are there the rich feel happy and proud. This kind of social dynamics was not questioned for several centuries and was accepted as a norm. The higher caste groups found these norms advantageous to them and so they never bothered about the discrimination meted out to the Dalits.

Normally the initiative for change that the Dalits are to be treated as normal human beings will not come from the higher caste communities. We also find with some of the lower castes under Sudra *Varna* just above the Dalits in the hierarchy though they are equally poor and sometimes below the level of living of the Dalits enjoy a sense of superiority over the Dalits. Economically they may be poor but the sense of caste status they enjoy is not what they earned. It is socially and traditionally passed on attribute or status to them. They may be farm workers along with the Dalits but in their interactions and especially with the Dalits and the way they address the Dalit women and men are different. Singular way of calling in the local language has two dimensions. Intimate people may address each in singular. When a speaker or a caller addresses or calls Dalit men and women in singular it means the caller is superior and the called is inferior. In English 'you' stands both as singular and plural but it is different in Telugu, Tamil, Kannada and Hindi. The way of addressing the upper castes show that they try to maintain their superior social status. But of late, slight changes are visible among the higher castes vis-à-vis the Dalits.

The conditions of the Dalits are an open book. This is one area of knowledge known to all the people in India. The exception may be a certain percentage of younger generation on both sides. We may briefly look into the approaches or measures to be adopted towards ameliorating their pitiable living conditions i.e. among the majority of Dalits. The approach here is a composite one comprising political, economic, social, educational, psychological and in a generic sense cultural and value system.

POLITICAL

The measures under the political domain are already there. This is in respect to certain percentage of reservations in constitutional administrative bodies such as Village Panchayats, Mandal Parishads, Zilla Parishad, State Legislatures and Parliament. Here we mention the first recognition and importance accorded to the Dalits was through elections. They were sought as voters and slowly the Dalits could recognise and realise their importance as voters with equality with everyone.

ECONOMIC

It may be noted here that both the Central and State Government have come out with some economic measures in terms of allocation of land, funds for housing, loans for petty business and allocation of house sites.

SOCIAL

Under social dimension the first and most important act was abolition of untouchability. It is a revolutionary measure which gave social position and recognition to the Dalits and created a kind of fear and anguish among the higher caste groups. We may also mention here certain reasonable percentage of reservation for Dalits in respect to admissions to educational institutions and jobs under union and State Service Commissions. One could see the legal consequences to the higher caste people when they address the Dalits as 'Mala' and 'Madiga'. The moment the aggrieved Dalit reports to the police, the person who has called the individual Dalit as 'Mala' or 'Madiga' will be immediately taken to the police custody. Aggrieved person need not produce any witness and the police also do not require any witness. The word or statement of the affected person is taken as truth. This aspect has in a short time brought in visible changes among higher caste groups and Dalits.

The problem mainly is in rural areas. For generations together the higher caste groups maintained social distance from the Dalits. Party based political activities slowly bring these two segments closer and a minimal intermixing of higher castes and Dalits is taking place. The field studies indicate both on the part of the caste Hindus and Dalits hesitation and some kind of inhibition on the part of the Dalits. Even though in schools and other educational institutions, the children of the caste Hindus and Dalits sit together, they interact in subtle ways. The children of the caste Hindus treat and behave differently with the children of the Dalits.

EDUCATIONAL

When it comes to literacy and education, literacy among the Dalits is low especially among women. The case studies included in the book show reluctance on the part of the parents and even among children attending school and pursuing higher education to go beyond X standard. One finds a small percentage of Dalit men and women going in for collegiate education, since as mentioned above there is reservation for the Dalit candidates positions in administrative system. It acts as an impetus and motivator for some Dalit candidates to go in for professional courses like Medicine and Engineering Technology. It is not a question of prediction that even to reach 50% of literacy on the part of Dalit men and women it may take a few decades.

PSYCHOLOGICAL

It is a subtle field. It is in the mind of the individual and his attitude. This attitude or the mindset stands for higher caste groups as well as the Dalits. So long the Dalits feel inferior and the higher caste groups maintain their superiority complex and do not receive the traditionally expected conduct or behaviour on the part of the Dalits, the upper caste individuals feel hurt and angry. But here in the case of Dalit men and women who occupy higher posts as Ministers, I.A.S., I.P.S. etc. Officers the way they are treated outwardly is different. The inward feeling or the attitude on the part of the caste Hindu colleagues or subordinates is different. Internally or mentally they go with the same social distance vis-à-vis the Dalit Officers. Growth or emergence of social equality would be a long journey.

CULTURE AND VALUE SYSTEM

Culture speaks of the way of life of people. Value system of any culture group is built over generations with additional and deletional elements. The value system of a group is reflected in their beliefs, rituals in respect to all important functions of life especially commensal relations and matrimonial alliances or intercaste, inter ethnic marriages. It is well neigh impossible to remodel or restructure a social group especially institution of caste in India. One has to accept unwillingness on the part of the higher caste groups and in a large number of cases the inhibition and inferiority complex and hesitant movement on the part of the Dalits. Equity and justice would advocate all-round efforts with concerted action which would remedy the Dalits from their economic poverty and social-suffocation.

It is known all over the world the initiative and the campaign carried on by Mahatma Gandhi against the practice of untouchability and calling the Dalits as 'Harijans' i.e. the children of Hari, Vishnu. In a sporadic way here and there some enlightened souls fought for the upliftment and welfare of the Dalits. The way in which the Dalits are treated is not segmental but a universal phenomenon in India. The awakening has to come among people who still hold on to unjustified, irreligious and ungodly behaviour towards the Dalits.

Caste differences were accepted as cultural and social norms and the way the Dalits are to be treated and interacted with so long. The social suffocation endured by the Dalits was not challenged, it flourished. Had it been challenged in the earlier centuries, it would have crumbled long ago. Many factors made the institution of caste thrive for a pretty long period. This winding has been going on for centuries and to unwind the whole thing in a matter of few decades would demand a basic change in people's attitudes. Caste lies in the mind of man. Let us hope that atleast in the years and decades to come the Dalits are treated as human beings worthy of respect and recognition.

CHAPTER 8

Programme Planning to Meet People's Needs

"Good Programmes result from the joint efforts of the technically trained workers and progressive villagers."

Though the rural development programme is of general and a comprehensive nature in terms of its focus, in this context we would like to emphasise on the development of Dalits in the country with the same kind of approach. In terms of development and the strategies to be applied does not vary in general from community to community. The same philosophy, the methodology and the ways of approach in respect to the downtrodden, the Dalit community all over the country requires methodically same approach with serious and religious dedication to this task. In the following pages we will briefly look into the way to go over planning for the development of Dalits. Whether you speak of a single community or ethnic group or the generality of multiple type of communities in the context of Indian variegated and diversified social structure the same principles and approach stand as means of understanding and bringing about changes to facilitate the onward movement of the Dalit community. When you speak of approaches to rural development, the same principles and approach apply to the development of the Dalits in the country.

In the following pages we discuss in general the approaches to rural development in terms of planning for action. Rural development programmes are created and maintained for influencing people to make changes in their way of living and of making a living. The existence of such programmes implies that the present situation of the rural people is not what it should and could be, that something different should prevail, and that it is possible through appropriate action to attain a more desirable status for them. From this assumption another one arises: that it is possible and feasible for a person or group of persons – officials, non-officials or a combination of both – to identify the nature of new conditions that could and should prevail, and devise means for achieving them. Hence, the entire process of planning for rural development implies a need for change. The question then arises: change from *what,* to *what,* by *whom, where* and *by what methods?*

Changes that are important to people are those that help them meet their needs for biological, economic, social, aesthetic and moral well-being. Basically, all programmes for rural development exist to help people meet their needs. If programmes do not do this, people in free-choice societies will not participate in them. The element of people's needs, therefore, becomes a central concern of planners for rural development. If a society is to find ways to adjust itself so that people meet their needs for an improved economic status, for being more useful citizens and for enjoying a higher degree of social satisfaction, it must identify these conditions and plan realistically to achieve them.

What needs do people have? How can needs be identified? What plan of priority should be set up for meeting people's needs? What resources are necessary to meet people's needs? How should resources be organized and directed to help people meet their needs? These questions give the key orientation and justification for rural programme planning.

THE NATURE AND ROLE OF PLANNING

The controlling objective of India's Rural Development Programmes is to develop in village people the ability to make a better living and to live a more satisfying life as individuals, as family members and as citizens of their community, state and nation. How to attain this objective is the key problem confronting the architects and current leaders of the scheme.

The first step in any systematic attempt to promote rural development is to prepare a useful programme. The term programme indicates focus, priority and design. It assumes the ability among the planners to distinguish important needs from unimportant ones. Such a programme must be based on people's needs to make it significant and on their interests to make it effective. *"If we could but know where we are now, and where we ought to go, we could better judge what to do, and how to do it"*. This statement by Abraham Lincoln lies at the heart of the nature and role of planning for rural development. Effective programmes for rural improvement do not just happen; they have to be built. Planning does not go on in a vacuum, or automatically; it has to be made to happen. Good programmes are not developed merely by wishing for them, but by working for them.

The need for planning arises from the complexity and from the importance of the job to be done. Planning is a necessary aspect of any activity that is too involved to be disposed of off-hand. The use of planning is to discover and prepare the way for action that should be taken. Planning gives meaning and system to action. It prepares the basis for a course of future action. Possibly, the most basic fact-giving rise to planning is that effective rural development results from choice, not from chance; it results from design, not from drift; it results from a plan; not by trial and error. Hence, effective work is an intentional effort carefully designed to attain certain specific and predetermined goals assumed to be important.

The use of programme planning stems from a belief in the need for change that results in progress, and from the view that change in certain directions is good for those affected by it. Planning must, therefore, result in programmes that help people find more satisfactory modes of living and of making a living. Planning assumes that the programme, or the lack of one, followed in the past will not do the job in the present and the future.

Designing programmes for rural development is one of the most difficult tasks confronting rural development workers. This is so because planners must avoid programming that has superimposed characteristics and instead assure programmes that have roots among the people. The problem is complex because the components of rural programming are complex. People, their needs, their interests, useful technology, educational process, analysing situations, making decisions about what should be done, determining useful action, projecting the desired shape of things into the future and such other components of rural programming are rarely simple. Programme planning for rural development has but little research support, a wide range of patterns of approach, and consequently requires great imagination and judgement on the part of the planners.

Good programme planning is primarily an intellectual activity, for it usually involves a study and use of facts and principles. It requires knowledge, imagination and reasoning ability. Often it requires a mastery over special skills and techniques of research. It is basically a process of making decisions that will carry into the future. If these decisions are not made wisely, they may not lead to useful attainment. Decisions have to be made about what the present situation is, how it could and ought to be changed and what means can be used to accomplish the new and more desirable situation. Finally, good planning for rural development requires the ability to synthesize facts and value judgements in a process of sound decision-making about the objectives the programmes should seek to attain and what courses of action are most likely to achieve them. The ability to plan requires:

1. an understanding of the nature and function of planning,
2. skill in formulating planning procedures,
3. skill in identifying problems and needs,
4. ability to decide on significant objectives and goals,
5. skill to formulating means and wise courses of action to attain objectives, and
6. skill in involving key leaders in the planning process.

The first condition of success for any programme to promote rural development is a widespread belief in the usefulness to a large number of people. Good plans are to the professional rural worker what the compass is to the seaman.

SOME GUIDES TO PLANNING

The broad aims set forth for India's Community Development Programme are great and important. They are complex and far-reaching. They are significant and difficult to achieve. But they are assumed to be worthy of effort, since foremost in the order of things they embody are social, economic and human values to which the new India is committed. The process through which these aims were derived was a long and tedious one involving many people, much study, interpretation of facts and careful application of judgment in arriving at final decisions. In short, a massive programme-planning job was done. Plans for rural development are usually made best when a number of propositions are followed in the planning process.

1. *Effective rural development programmes must have clear and significant objectives*

An objective is that which a person, group or agency sets before itself as an object or condition to be attained. Programme objectives designate directions of movement. Since that is so, objectives properly become the focus of primary material and human resources for attaining change. Maximum progress can be made only when the objectives are clear, full commitment of resources is made to achieving them and effective use is made of the resources.

If there is to be progress and not mere evolution in the development of people, the objectives of the programme must be clearly and periodically determined in view of progress and changed conditions. It should be kept in mind that not all people need or desire to move in the same direction or for the same distances. Directions have varying degrees of importance to different people. Extension workers must be prepared to offer opportunity for people to move in various directions. This is what is really meant by the term-balanced programme. Thus, a good programme objective is one that provides possible direction for large numbers of people to move some distance, a direction in which they want and need to move, then provide them assistance in travelling in those directions. This is really the essence of extension work for Community Development.

These facts place great importance on the wise choice of purposes. For, if the choice of purposes is not made well, the resources committed to their attainment will be poorly used. This is a mistake the leaders of India's rural development scheme can ill afford to make, especially at a time like the present when the objectives to be achieved are so numerous and so great and resources for achieving them so few and so small.

2. ***To achieve the broad purposes of Community Development requires planning at the top level and also at lower levels including the state, district, Block and village.***

Deciding purposes at these lower levels requires a degree of specificity that results in objectives being moved from the level of glittering generality to the level of practical reality. Identifying the most useful purposes, assigning a priority to them and developing effective means of achieving them at the local level is an intricate process which must ebb handled with great skill. If the statement of purposes at higher levels is to be realistic and useful in guiding the programme at lower levels, it must be reformulated at each lower level to align it with varying situations.

3. ***There are no unplanned programmes.***

Programme development is a relative matter. The quality of a programme is related to the extent to which certain steps are taken that are essential in planning. A number of crucial questions about programming must be asked and their answers taken into account in the planning process. Proper answers to them will improve the preciseness with which programmes are developed. These questions are:

a) To whom and to how many people is the programme important?

b) In what way is the programme significant to people – economically, socially, aesthetically, or morally?

c) What is the relative importance of programme objectives?

d) Who thinks the programme is important – nation, state, district, block, village?

e) Who arrived at the programme objectives?

f) On what amounts and kinds of information is the programme based?

g) Does the programme reflect significant needs and interest of large numbers of people?

h) Who is acquainted with the programme and its purposes?

i) How clearly conceived and understood is the programme by those who are to participate in its execution?

j) What would be the likely consequences in one, five or ten years if work on certain parts of the programme is not carried out?

4. ***The most effective rural development programmes result when there is general agreement among village, block, district, state and national officials on three important items.***

Village and block workers in order to plan the most effective programmes need to agree on (a) a basic philosophy regarding programme development, (b) a clear policy that reflects the basic philosophy, and (c) a workable procedure that gives general direction but provides ample latitude for adjustments needed to meet local situations. Questions like the following may serve as a guide for this purpose:

a) What is the relative importance of programme development as a step in the rural development process?

b) Who should participate in programme development and in what way?

c) How much time should be allocated to the task of planning?

d) Should a so-called long-range programme be developed in each village and block?

e) Upon what kinds and amounts of factual information should the programme be based and how should this information be collected?

f) To what extent should procedures provide for participation of people at the village and block level?

g) Should the different phases of a block programme be organized into a single overall unified programme?

h) What is the role of the technical specialist in block and village programme development?

i) To what extent should leaders among the villagers participate and which method is most useful for providing this opportunity?

In relation to these questions there are many different points of view depending on established policy and other factors. But experience and sound principles of good programming suggest that such questions should be considered with care. One point of view suggests that when numerous problems are evident, as in Indian villages, decisions are easily made about what should be done. This argument has validity. But merely making decisions about what should be done is not enough. Also important is how the decisions are made, on what facts are they based, who participates in making them and what priority is to be followed in meeting the needs.

5. ***Programmes are most effective when based on adequate and current facts pertaining to local conditions as well as those related to national and regional situations.***

No rural development programme or any of its parts can be any better than the facts on which it is based. A programme must be based on adequate and current facts about the situation at all levels and related factors that influence it in order to be most effective. To be useful, these facts must finally be carefully analyzed and interpreted through the joint efforts of the technically trained staff and progressive village leaders. Facts about the local situation and others affecting it form the foundation upon which the Block staff and village leaders, working on various community development problems, build and carry out an effective programme. When properly weighed on the scales of people's values, these facts reflect local needs and the enlightened desires of people. Moreover, they show not only what people think they want, but also what is best for them. To define rural problems it is necessary to consider both scientific and folk knowledge. Thus, the true basis for a programme lies in the needs and problems of the individual, the home, the farm and the community.

The fact cannot be overstressed that local conditions furnish the basic problems with which rural development programmes must deal. People are most concerned about facts relating to their immediate situation as it affects them personally. Community development workers and local leaders use properly interpreted facts about local conditions to show how these facts directly and personally affect the people. In this way interest is aroused and indications found that lead to the solution to problems. Facts about the local situation help to identify problems and needs with which the people are concerned by pointing out the gaps between what is and what should be, by indicating shortages and by drawing attention to undesirable trends. To have adequate facts about a local situation, data that generally fall into these four categories must be obtained.

a) Current trends and outlook.

b) The people themselves – their needs, interests, knowledge, social organization, etc.

c) Physical factors about agriculture, industry, health, sanitation, etc.

d) Community problems – communication, education, etc.

6. *Selection of a relatively small number of the most significant needs singled out for major attention contributes to the effectiveness of rural development programmes.*

When the resources for promoting rural development are limited, a programme cannot successfully be at the same time all things to all people. To identify problems or needs that are important is a relatively easy task, but it is not enough. Problems must be found that are not only important but that are most important. Consequently, some careful choice-making must be done. Since it is physically impossible to deal simultaneously with all the needs of people in a block or village, it is necessary to sort out for special attention those needs that are of greatest importance at a given time, thus developing a scheme of priority for dealing with items in the programme. Programme elements may then be arranged according to relative amounts of time and other resources committed to them. Research quite clearly supports the idea that no single exposure of a person to a recommendation will usually produce much action. Getting the adoption of new practices generally requires that recommendations be brought to people's attention on several occasions spread over a period of time. It is necessary then, in cooperation with village leaders, to ferret out the most significant problems and weave them into the core of a vital and dynamic village and block development programme. The most significant problems can then be attacked with all the resources of the programme which collectively form a powerful force for economic and social change.

7. *Skilful involvement of progressive village leaders is fundamental in planning rural development programmes.*

A synthesis of experience in planning rural programmes makes it clear that programmes developed *with*, not *for* or *by* the people, stand the best chance of success. Good programmes result from joint efforts of the technically trained development workers and the progressive members of the villages. The key to successful programme development, therefore, lies in weaving the following information together into decisions about what should be done: facts about local conditions, targets set up at national, state and regional levels, knowledge of block and village staff and that of local and village leaders.

This is a vastly complex task and one of the most important jobs and greatest challenges to better programming and, in turn, to more effective Community Development. There are many reasons that make constant work at this task worthwhile. In the first place, "it is not what the programme does for people but what it does *to* them that counts." Secondly, the assumption is very unsound that either the village leaders alone, or officials at the block, district or national level alone, have all the good ideas about what the programme should be. Good programmes should reflect the best knowledge and insights of *both* village leaders and professionally trained workers.

Furthermore, good planning procedures lead people to see beyond the present felt needs to the basic underlying problems. The ultimate performance must be by the people; for it is what they do that is of transcendent importance. It is clear, therefore, that rural development programmes – if they are to have their roots in the social and economic life of villagers – must be planned in villages and blocks around the needs and interests of the people. Programmes planned in this way become programmes of the people, with all the pride of authorship and satisfaction that comes from joint participation in both their planning and in execution.

All village people, of course, cannot be involved in this process. The problem of people's participation is handled by tuning in the masses through carefully selected village leaders. To attain worthwhile goals there usually must be some compromise between the ideal and the practical – between facts and value judgments. Is there any better way of assuring this than by involving village leaders with the block staff in analyzing situations and in making the decision on what should be done to improve conditions?

8. *Programmes that are planned for longer periods of time than one or two years tend toward greater effectiveness.*

Long-time programming, or identifying objectives that aim into the future, is more likely to be effective for a number of reasons. The important needs of people usually cannot be met in the short period of one or two years. Changing what people believe, what they do, and how they do it, is, at best, a slow process. Long and constant effort is usually needed to accomplish important community development objectives. To assure continued work on the most fundamental needs in a village or block requires provision in the programme for important elements to recur periodically. The formation of long-time objectives is a good technique for assuring continuation of work that focuses on major needs. This point of view suggests that care should be taken in the planning process to provide assurance that the short-term interests of people are also to their long-time advantage.

9. *Procedures in rural programming that assure fairly close integration of problems related to the farm, the home and the community appear to contribute to their soundness and effectiveness.*

The word integration implies a smooth and efficient operation of a combination of activities or services in the solution of problems. In view of the wide scope of content in a community development programme and the common objectives of its phases, various aspects of the programme should be blended into one effective force aimed at building better rural communities. The primary way to achieve coordination and integration in programmes is through common understanding among officials as well as between them and non-officials. This can be attained most effectively through joint participation in appropriate phases of the planning process.

10. *Programme planning must take into account cultural values and the social system.*

Rural development programmes cannot be most effective unless they are planned and carried out in harmony with the basic cultural values held by people and the social setting in which they live. Cultural values reflect what people generally think is important. The social system tends to maintain adherence to the scale of established values. In traditional cultures, the social system and prevailing cultural values tend to serve as forces working against social and economic reform. Even in so-called advanced societies these influences are formidable. Programmes, therefore, cannot be most successful when they are too much at odds with innovations the value system will sanction. People's values and their social system must be understood and taken into account by planners of rural development programmes.

11. Programme content must be determined with care and preciseness.

Predictions with a high degree of accuracy can be made about the probable outcome of programmes to promote change by examining their content. Content specifies the subject areas in which change is expected to be made. Consequently, the content of programmes is the most important index to new ways in which people may be influenced to behave. Programme content represents what actually will be attempted in changing people and the situation in which they live. Methods used for executing programmes are merely means to ends, not the ends themselves. The selection of the content of programmes of change tends, therefore, to be a central or basic concern in rural programme planning.

12. The interpretation of the programme to officials and non-officials and to the general public is an essential step in successful programming.

It is important that the aims and objectives of programmes become common knowledge among villagers. Interpretation means translating into familiar language or into terms that are readily understood as well as explanation of the meaning of facts as they apply to local conditions. Interpretation is important, for, unless people know what is available to them they cannot know what kind of help to request for.

PROFESSIONAL ABILITIES NEEDED BY PLANNERS

Planning effective programmes for Community Development requires a number of high-level professional skills. Needed abilities include understanding and skill in at least the following broad areas of competency:

1. Understanding of the nature and role of the Rural Development Services.
2. Knowledge and understanding of technology related to subjects with which the programme is to deal.
3. Ability to clarify the objectives of a programme and to state them so that they are useful in guiding its execution.
4. Ability to organize people and things.
5. Skill at seeing the relationship between principles and practice.
6. Skill at inquiry.
7. Skill in human relations.

In the following pages, a brief characterization is made of each of these areas of competency. If the suggestions made here provide some insight and serve as useful guides to further study, they will serve their purpose.

1. Understanding of the nature and role of the multi-faceted Rural Development Programme.

Gaining an understanding of the nature of the services extended in India and its role as a national initiative for promoting rural development, requires a knowledge of the following:

a) Development, present scope, philosophy and objectives of Community Development.
b) Organization and administration of the agency at the national, state, district, block and village levels.
c) The role of various categories of personnel at various levels in the hierarchy.
d) Responsibility and opportunity of the agency in a developing country.

Adequate competency in these areas is fundamental to effectiveness and leadership on the part of officials and non-officials in the entire organization. Each officer is a professional person. Knowing about one's professional affiliation is commonly viewed as a primary tool of the trade in any field of endeavour. Without this knowledge one cannot understand one's job, intelligently defend his profession, or suggest action to improve it. Likewise, he cannot effectively communicate opportunities to those who should participate. Effective professional leadership requires competency in this area on the part of all personnel engaged in the programme.

2. *Knowledge and understanding of technology related to subjects with which the programme is to deal.*

Adequate knowledge and understanding of technology appropriate to one's professional job requires the following:

a) Thoroughness of knowledge.

b) Acquaintance with current technology.

c) Knowledge of reliable sources of technology.

d) Understanding of how technology relates to specific problems.

e) Continuous study.

Technology related to the various special fields with which Community Development is concerned constitutes the chief commodity the programme has to offer to people. Whether the subject is agricultural production, social education, cooperatives, home science, youth work or any other, a body of useful technology is assumed to be available. Every successful educational effort requires significant technology appropriate to the problems dealt with. Subject-matter or technology is to workers in rural development what food is to human beings; it is life's sustenance. To attempt to teach others something one does not know oneself is to invite failure from the start. Every official in the community development organization, therefore, should have not only adequate knowledge of appropriate technology in his particular field of operation, but also an understanding of it and its relationship to the problems of villagers.

3. Ability to clarity objectives of a programme and state them so that they are useful in guiding its execution.

The importance and role of programme objectives were mentioned previously. The ability to clarify and state objectives for one's work is also important. This task includes:

a) An understanding of the nature of purpose and the role of objectives in educational work.

b) Knowledge of the sources of objectives.

c) Knowledge of levels and interrelation of objectives.

d) Skill in stating and using objectives to guide educational activity.

It has been said that 'to him who knows not the port to which he is bound, no wind can be favourable.' A frequent criticism of workers in Community Development is related to the fuzziness with which objectives are conceived and stated. Too often statements of objectives at all levels can be characterized as glittering generalities. In this form they are not very helpful in guiding the programme. The importance of clarifying objectives and goals is found in two major truths:

a) Subject-matter and methods necessary to attain educational goals can be wisely selected only when the objectives are specific and clearly stated.

b) Evidence of the effectiveness of community development work can be collected only in the light of specific and clearly defined objectives.

Clear objectives, therefore, improve the preciseness with which educational activity is carried on. One important characteristic of the twenty first century is its requirement of decisiveness in action. Clear objectives give direction to action.

4. Ability to organize people and things.

This requires an understanding of:

a) The nature and function of organization.

b) Principles of organization.

c) Techniques of organization.

d) The nature and role of coordination and integration in programmes.

The need for organization increases in direct ratio to the growth in the size and complexity of tasks to be performed by an individual or an agency in attaining its purposes. Organization is properly viewed as an arrangement of relationships of persons or functions. It should be looked upon as a means, not as an end. The principle of organization is not limited in its application to people alone, but has a much broader application. People are organized for joint activity. Materials, ideas and facts are organized for common use or for use by one person. Thinking is essentially a process of organizing facts and ideas with a view to taking action. In all cases, the need for organization has its origin in the work to be done. The term organization is properly used when it refers to any collection of persons, materials, procedures, ideas, facts and the like, so arranged and ordered that in each case the parts make a meaningful whole. Good organization then is that which groups activities ideas, facts, materials or persons so as to get the best performance with the least effort. Good organizational ability is shown by definite regularity, predictability and dependability in the everyday performance of persons or groups doing the job expected of them.

The act of organizing requires attention to at least the two following definite and well-established processes:

a) *Coordination*. Coordination means making harmonious adjustment – to give things and actions their proper perspective – to unify designated effort into an integrated whole. Coordination is necessary in carrying out practically any job or assignment. It, therefore, becomes the essence of any effective organization of efforts. There must be coordination in all major community development functions, including administration, supervision, programming, programme execution and appraisal of accomplishments.

b) *Procedure Analysis*. Procedure is a way of arranging sequences of operations necessary for effective action. Certain definite elements must always be considered and employed in both the preparation and evaluation of procedures. Important facts upon which the success of procedures rests must be discovered, selected and clarified. These are the facts which are of such outstanding importance that they must be given consideration in the design of procedures.

Organizational ability is a high level skill and is essential to the effectiveness of

extension workers.

5. ***Skill in seeing the relationship between principle and practice.***

The ability to relate principle and practice involves knowledge and understanding of::

a) The nature and role of principles related to Community Development.

b) The nature and role of techniques and procedures for carrying out programmes.

c) The inseparable interdependence of principle and practice in the extension educational process.

Theory and practice always have a relationship. Principles relate to why, techniques to how. One may understand the structure of theory and be unable to apply it in practice. On the other hand, one may be able to use technique skilfully, but be superficial in one's efforts because one does not understand how the technique relates to the whole process of Community Development, or to the specific aspect of the activity one is performing.

The effective extension worker is neither only an abstract thinker nor only an accomplished user of tricks. He is both. He must understand the principle lying behind his technique in order to make the technique most effective. The importance of principles stems from the fact that they are general rules – well established truths – that usually have wide application. They serve as useful guides in a wide range of situations. Extension workers equipped with an understanding of principles applicable to their work are more likely to be creative than those who pride themselves on just being practical.

Rural development, workers sometimes appear to misinterpret the term 'practical'. They infer that to be practical, things must be simple, easy to do, primer-like, not complicated. The basic meaning of the term practical really suggests that whatever technique works well in a situation, regardless of its complexity, is practical. Principles give meaning to technique. Techniques give application to principles. One who glorifies techniques without trying to understand the principles related to them is really a captive of technique. One who paramounts principles without an understanding of the technique necessary to apply them are a captive of theory. An understanding of principles related to techniques and skill with techniques is the height of professional competency. The person who only knows how and the person who only knows why are always likely to have a job, but the person who knows both how and why will eventually supervise both of them.

6. Skill at inquiry.

Ability at inquiry requires the following skills necessary to help individuals:

a) Identify their problems,

b) Discover focal points of concern,

c) Determine alternative solutions, and

d) Evaluate possible solutions and make decisions about them.

Without this competency, extension workers cannot be effective in helping people analyze their problems. Skill at inquiry is not only basic to planning, but also to guidance. Unless rural development workers are skilful at inquiry they cannot help people discover problems and work out useful solutions to them. It is a relatively easy task to supply answers based on opinion, but a vastly more difficult one to supply leadership that truly helps others analyze their problems and arrive at sound decisions about them. The process of inquiry consists of these four primary steps:

a) Identifying the difficulty or problem or need. Inquiry usually begins with a specific problem that causes people to feel that something ought to be done. Whenever a situation causes people – officials or non-officials – to be disturbed, there is need for inquiry, community-wide, family-wide or confined to an individual. Those responsible for planning rural development programmes should be skilful in discovering these feelings of dissatisfaction in order to further analyze the special aspects of the situation in which ***lies*** the specific concern.

b) *Discovering the focal point of trouble.* This step requires facts that will pinpoint the true nature of a problem, its scope and its importance. It usually entails careful scrutiny of attitudes, beliefs, values, habits, prejudices and the like, in addition to the scrutiny of the body of information commonly called facts.

c) *Determining possible ways to solve the problems.* In this step, ideas about plans of action must be developed that offer possible solutions to the difficulty. At this point, community development workers must provide leadership. Often it is easy to supply solutions to problems, but difficult to reach a truly joint decision about how to solve them.

d) *Evaluating alternative plans of actions.* This step requires the ability to project probable consequences of each suggested course of action if it were taken. It involves determining the probable value of each idea, and a decision about which kind of action is most likely to succeed.

Without skill at inquiring, a rural worker's relation with the people is one of the blind leading the blind, or, even the more disastrous one of the blind attempting to lead those with excellent sight.

7. *Skill in human relations.*

Ability in human relations is necessary for successful work with people in general, and especially with local leaders, co-workers and those in the administrative organization.

Human relations concern how people get along with one another. Since the job of extension workers is ultimately to bring about educational change in people, they have to discover how to get people act in the ways they want them to. If extension workers cannot do this, they must change their goals to those desired by the people. If rural development workers cannot bring what they want in line with what people want, they may as well give up trying to change people in that particular way. One may know the technical answer, but unless one also knows how to work with people one won't know how to get technical answers translated into better farm, home, and community practices.

Man not having been born a social being, these behaviours have to be learned. Fortunately, they can be developed. Human judgement is fallible and mistakes will always be made. But many errors in relations among people can be avoided if fundamentals of the subject are studied and understood.

"A CONCEPT OF "NEEDS"

Efforts to promote change in conditions of free-choice participation are successful only to the extent they are focused on the important needs of people and are effective in helping people meet these needs. Under voluntary conditions of participation, people concern themselves with programmes of change only when they think that the programme is valuable to them in meeting personal, family, group or community needs, therefore, becomes a central concern in rural programming.

Since the people in Indian villages are free to participate in community development activity or not to participate, their participation in effect constitutes casting a vote. When they participate, they vote favourably. When they do not participate, they also vote, but unfavourably. They determine their vote on the basis of their estimate of the probable value to them of the things participation may give them. This judgement is made on the basis of satisfaction, or the lack of it – economic, social, aesthetic or moral – which a villager feels he may obtain from participation. In short, people concern themselves with programmes only on the basis of needs as they see them, not as the officials view them. The central problem, therefore, of successful programming is one of identifying accurately what people want, think they need, and actually do need, and then getting these items woven into a realistic well organized and concerted series of forceful activities. This may properly be called a programme. Effective programmes to promote change are developed through an approach to individuals and groups – by finding people's needs and arranging action that helps meet them. Hence, a clear understanding of the nature and role of people's needs in programmes of change is essential to the leaders of such programmes.

The term need is a simple four-letter word and appears rather innocent at a glance. But it is one of the most important words related to rural development programmes. This is so because the needs of people constitute the core around which successful programmes are built. Needs imply conditions including necessity, requirement, urgency, prerequisite, vacancy, scarcity, lack and indispensability. An understanding of the nature and role of people's needs can be developed by gaining a clear concept of the meaning and implications of a number of widely accepted propositions related to the term need. Some basic aspects of need are indicated as follows:

1.Man is an independent living system surrounded by an environment with which he constantly interrelates.

Man is constantly influenced by his environment and in turn exerts influence over it. His well-being depends on keeping a balance between the internal forces produced by the energy resulting from the food intake and the external conditions produced by the environment. To keep the human system in equilibrium with the external forces, it is necessary that certain needs be met. In this sense every person is continuously meeting his needs – trying to attain those conditions of living that make for satisfaction. To the extent that the relationship between man and his environment goes out of balance, he has needs. People are constantly attempting to attain, maintain or improve this balance.

The nature and extent of needs depend upon the nature and extent of the imbalance. For example, when a person becomes physically ill, a condition is created in which the affected parts of the body become functionally out of balance with the other parts. Consequently, it is said that the person is sick. To get well, the imbalance must be removed. In a like manner the imbalance between man and his environment in all of its aspects is the source from which people's needs emerge. Man's attempt to attain, and maintain a satisfying equilibrium between internal and external forces represents in a true form his real struggle for survival and economic, social, aesthetic or moral improvement.

2. ***People's needs are identified by finding through the programme planning process, the actual, the possible and the valuable.***

By the actual is meant *what is;* by the possible is meant *what could be* and by the valuable is meant *what ought to be.* In choosing the things on which to focus programmes, it is necessary to analyze these conditions and possibilities and choose from among them the *most valuable.* Then it should become the objective of programmes to change people and the present conditions in which they live to the most valuable and possible conditions. Making the analyses and decisions necessary in this context is the essence of programme planning to meet people's needs.

3. ***People's needs may be defined as the differences between what is, what could be and what ought to be.***

Needs always imply a gap between the two conditions as shown in the following diagram:

WHAT OUGHT TO BE

(Desirable situation)

↕	GAP (Need) Difference, dearth, vacancy, requirement, urgency	↕

WHAT IS

(Actual situation)

W*hat is* can be determined by a study of the situation. Some of the major kinds of information this study should include are important facts about people, their attitudes, knowledge, and what they think their needs are. It should include facts about physical factors, soils, crops, livestock, home conditions, farm implements, production resources and community services. It should include facts about public problems, programmes, trends and outlook.

What ought to be can be determined on the basis of research findings and value judgements of the people and their official leaders. For example, the results of research may show that the use of recommended practices in rice production will result in a one-third larger yield per acre. The cultivator on the other hand, may not place great value on reaching this level of production, or he may place greater value on spending his available resources on some other goal like better education for his children than on producing extra rice.

It should be recognized that information about *what is* does not make a programme, it only shows the situation. From this point planners have to take another step. This step is that of deciding *what ought to be*- what the desirable situation is. Hence, deciding on *what ought to be* is the process of selecting programme targets, goals or objectives. In setting objectives, care must be taken to assure that the level of *what ought to be* is within the physical, economic, social and mental possibilities of attainment by those who are expected to make the change. Finally, it should be recognized that the nature and extent of the need (the width of the gap) is an indication of the significance of the problem. The wider the gap, the greater the problem.

4. ***People have to recognize the gap between the actual, the possible and the desirable and place value on attaining the desirable condition before they will become motivated to change in desirable directions.***

This point poses the crux of the problem in programmes of change. Village people being wedded to custom and tradition, often being illiterate and surrounded by many outmoded cultural norms, are slow to make innovations in what they do and how they do it. When people have been schooled by centuries of experience to satisfy their wants by not having wants, it is difficult to conceive them that they should, for example, adopt new practices to increase crop yields or go through the uncertainties of consolidating several tracts of land into one piece.

Reluctance by villagers to change is not due altogether to a natural resistance to change, but to an apparent lack of interest in change. They seem to feel satisfied with their old ways even when new ones are demonstrated side by side with the old. When the actual or *status quo* is seen as the ideal, desirable or satisfactory status of things, no need is recognized on the part of people. Consequently, there is in their minds no need for a programme to promote change because there is no need for change in the first place, as they view the situation. To be successful, therefore, a programme must cause people to recognize the gap between the actual, the desirable and the possible, and place a value on attaining the desirable.

5. ***Human behaviour and the status of things can only be judged by some standard and the standard can only be derived from a concept of what is valuable and desirable to attain.***

Human behaviour and the status of things usually can be placed on a scale of human values.

The human values are dependant and influenced by geographic, climatic, historical, religious, ethnic, occupational, contact with other cultures, colonization and density or thinness of population. The values are not constant but they are dynamic. They are related and sometimes-unrelated elements lived by the people at a given point of time. Speaking of values, some may remain especially of religious nature constant but food habits, dress and technology may change over a period of time.

From a psychological standpoint, needs may be classified into two groups, viz., felt or consciously recognized needs and *unfelt* or unrecognized needs. In a free society all needs must become felt before they serve as motivating forces. Research in adult education indicates that adults often are not aware of many of their most important needs. To the extent that this is true, adults have needs which are unfelt. Significant needs of which people are not conscious must be ferreted out and met in order to help them advance toward more desirable economic and social conditions.

One of the problems in rural programming, therefore, is to help people identify important needs they do not recognize. Thus it is not enough to base programmes entirely on what people feel their needs are, because these often may not represent some of their most important needs. Leaders of programmes must dig deep and identify needs people have which they do not recognize, then plan educational effort to convert these into felt needs. Without this, rural development programmes will be less significant and may tend to focus on the everyday short-term interests of people rather than on their more basic long-time needs.

6. ***Final decision about the selection, or rejection, of needs to be included in a programme should be made with great care.***

In the process of programme planning to meet people's needs, many decisions have to be made. These decisions have to be related to the actual, the valuable and the possible. Ultimately they must become decisions about acceptance or rejection of items to be included in the programme. These are crucial decisions and are highly significant, not only because the future of the people and their conditions will be influenced, but because extensive physical and human resources will be committed to helping people meet the needs accepted by planners and made a part of the programme. Indeed, these needs become the subject-matter or content of a programme. In turn, they are translated into the objectives or targets which the programme will seek to attain in course of time.

In the process of making final decisions about the needs to be included in a programme, some further points should be kept in mind. All people have needs. Needs vary in nature, scope and significance. Needs are often individual in attachment but they also tend to be common among members of groups. Needs change with time and progress. This tends to be true whether concerted effort is made to meet them or whether nothing is done to meet them. The needs of people change with age, growth and with social, economic and family status situations. People's needs arise from lack of harmony between themselves and their environment. The relative importance of needs is influenced by the physical environment, what is possible in it, and by the cultural factors which form a system of values that people hold to be important.

CRITERIA FOR PRACTICE AND PROCEDURE IN PROGRAMMING

The process of programme planning to meet people's needs includes four major elements or key steps that are generally viewed as of primary importance. It appears that the development staff should give proper attention to these elements in planning programmes that are significant and workable. The elements are:

a) A plan for involving local people in the planning process.

b) Procedure in programming planning.

c) The programme – the product of planning.

d) The annual plan of work.

These elements are described briefly in the following pages and a set of criteria for dealing with each of them is suggested. The criteria are attempts to describe the major steps, procedures or conditions that evidence shows to be good practice, involved in dealing with each element. The criteria are selected and designed to specify conditions, procedures, or practices that are conducive to developing the most effective rural programmes.

ELEMENT - A

A plan for involving people in programme planning

Rural programme planning, in essence, is a process of making decisions about important objectives to be attained in an area. One of the most significant problems confronting rural development workers is that of deciding on programme objectives which reflect the primary needs and interests of people. How to do this skillfully is a question of major concern to every professional worker. Decisions about programme objectives are usually best when made neither by the officials alone, nor by the people alone, but when made jointly by the officials and the people.

The contributions of the local people to rural programming are obtained most effectively through some form of organized approach. Research indicates that no one type of organization is best for programming in all situations. There are certain criteria, however, which are usually met when the local people contribute to programme development most effectively. These are indicated below:

1. Representative committees of non-officials are organized by the development staff. These function systematically on a continuing basis in developing and maintaining a current programme for development.
2. The people who function as members of the planning committees at the local level represent major interest groups, various economic and social levels of people, major vocations of the locality and other important elements in the area.
3. Each member of the planning groups clearly understands (a) the purpose of the group, (b) how the group can function in attaining its purpose, and (c) his individual role as a member of the group.
4. Members of the planning groups functioning at the local level are selected by appropriate democratic procedures.
5. Policies or rules formed for maintaining continuity of the planning groups include an appropriate plan for terminating the services of the temporary groups, and membership in the permanent groups, and for selecting new members of the permanent groups and new temporary groups.

ELEMENT - B

Procedure in programme planning

Procedure in programme planning means the process, course of action, methods, or major steps taken in an area to develop a suitable programme. A summary of experience of extension workers and conclusions from research pertaining to procedures used in rural programme development supports the following conclusions.

a) There are a number of essential steps in programme development that must be taken to develop a programme of the highest quality.

b) The basic steps are generally applicable with adjustments to meet particular circumstances in local situations.

c) After the steps are properly executed the basic principles of programme development should be applied.

d) The detailed procedures employed for executing each of the basic steps may vary considerably in accomplishing the purpose of each step.

The following is a list of criteria pertaining to the various steps assumed to be essential in procedures for local programme development.

1. The entire development staff has considered and reached agreement on:
   a) The importance to be attached to programming
   b) The amount of time to be devoted to programming
   c) The time when programming is to be done
   d) The phases of the programme to be developed, and
   e) The general approach to be followed in the area.
2. The development staff, with the help of technical specialists and planning groups, has assembled basic facts about the situation for use in developing a programme including such information as the following:
   a) Sources and levels of family income
   b) Health and educational levels of the people
   c) Needs and interests of the people

d) Marketing facilities and practices

e) Farming and home-making practices, and

f) Community problems and needs.

3. Basic facts about the local situation have been analyzed jointly by the official staff and the planning groups and decisions made on this basis about major needs and interests of people.
4. A long-term programme has been developed and is used as a guide to all major activity in the area.
5. The technical specialists have assisted in developing the long-term programme by supplying specific basic information and recommendations pertaining to their special field that has been considered by the staff and the planning groups.
6. The development staff, jointly with the planning groups, has defined the problem and taken decisions about the long-term and the short-term objectives of the programme in line with major needs and interests of the people.
7. The development staff, jointly with the planning groups, has arranged a system of priority for work on problems included in the long-term programme.
8. The planning groups along with the official staff, has actively promoted coordination of the long-term programme.

ELEMENT - C

The Programme

A rural development programme is a carefully prepared statement written in a form that clearly sets froth the significant changes that are needed in the behaviour of the people and in the conditions in which they live, to be attained over a period of time. Specifically, it is a statement that includes:

a) Primary facts that reveal the situation for each major subject or problem in the area that is to be dealt within the programme.

b) Significant problems or needs.

c) Major means for meeting the problems or needs.

d) Statement of long-term objectives to be attained.

It is of utmost importance that the staff and the people in each area not only develop a basic long-term programme, but also prepare the programme in a written form that is readily understood and is suitable for use as a guide for officials and non-officials. Experience shows that this practice is a valuable guide to the staff and advisory committees and also a very effective means of improving public relations. The criteria listed below represent standards that should be achieved in written statements of a basic long-term programme.

1. The written programme should be suitable for use by the staff, planning groups, and other individuals or groups concerned with the programme.
2. It should state the primary facts that clearly reveal the situation for major subject or problem areas.
3. It should clearly state the important problems or needs identified by the staff and the people in the programming process.
4. It should state both the long-term and short-term objectives for each major subject or problem area that is to be focused on in programme execution over a period of time.
5. It should state the objectives of the programme in a form that:
   a) Clearly reveals the kind of new condition or situation desired
   b) Is meaningful to the staff and the people, and
   c) Will serve as a useful guide to programme execution.
6. It should specify the subject-matter related to each objective that is highly significant to the people, socially or economically, or both.
7. It should include the summary of the long-term programme prepared in a form suitable for public distribution, containing the following items:

a) Major facts about the over-all area situation.
b) Brief statement of the organization, statements of major problems, long-term objectives, and major means of achieving them for each of the major subject or problem areas.
c) Brief descriptions of the situation, statements of major problems, long-term objectives, and major means of achieving them for each of the major subject or problem areas.
d) The names of members of the planning groups and the official staff, and
e) Other appropriate information.

8. It should be made available in a summary form to all the members of the planning groups, and the professional staff.
9. It should be circulated by appropriate means so that the general public can understand its nature and objectives.
10. It should be used as the basis for developing annual plans of work.

ELEMENT – D

The Annual Plan of Work

The annual plan of work commonly consists of a definite outline of procedure for carrying out work related to the different phases of the long-term programme. It should indicate specifically the means to be used and the methods of using them. Its basic function is to provide a guide for use in carrying on development work planned for the year in a systematic manner. The annual plan of work should effectively serve the following functions:

a) A specific guide for carrying out systematically all the major aspects of work planned for the year.
b) A guide to the development of plans and procedures for evaluating accomplishments.
c) A guide to the scheduling of activity related to various aspects of the programme.

The following criteria related to annual plans of work are assumed to be important in their development and use.

1. Annual plans of work should be developed and used as a guide to all major activity during the year.
2. They should be developed from the long-term programme in a way that the content and goals are directly in line with the objectives of the different phases of the long-term programme.
3. They should include facts about the current situation pertaining to major subject or problem areas assembled by the development staff, technical specialists, and planning groups. They should also include facts about accomplishments during the past year for consideration in developing the annual plan of work.
4. They should include decisions jointly taken by the staff and the planning group on the major problems to be worked on during the year after a careful analysis of the current facts.
5. An annual plan of work in a written form, prepared by the staff, includes the following kinds of information for each project, subject or problem area:
   a) Major subjects or problems to be worked on during the year.
   b) Goals to be attained during the year.
   c) Brief description of work to be done – methods, materials, etc.
   d) Who is to participate in carrying out the plan?
   e) A calendar of work which shows the approximate amount of time to be devoted to each major activity, and seasonal distribution of major activities.
   f) Who is to be reached with the programme?
6. The annual plan of work is used during the year as a basis for:
   a) Coordinating activities of the different aspects of the area programme.

b) Developing and coordinating teaching plans for different specific activities.

7. The annual plan of work is reproduced in an appropriate form for distribution and copies placed in the hands of (a) local leaders, (b) planning groups, and (c) other groups and individuals whose support is important for advancing the programme.

8. Means are used to acquaint the general public with the major activities to be undertaken during the year that is specified in the annual plan of work.

ORGANIZATION OF PROGRAMMES

Important changes in human behaviour generally are not produced quickly. Usually, no single learning experience has a very profound influence on people who participate in programmes. Changes in the ways of thinking, in fundamental habits, in attitudes, in interests, develop slowly. In free-choice societies, it is only after months and years that workers in rural development are usually able to see major changes resulting from their educational efforts. In some respects, the effect of programmes involving education is cumulative like that of water constantly dripping on a stone and wearing it away. In a day, or a week or a month, there is no appreciable change in the stone, but over a period of years definite erosion is noted.

Correspondingly, by the accumulation of impressions resulting from exposure to recommendations made by rural development workers, profound changes are brought about in the action of rural people. In order that educational effort produces cumulative effect, it must be so organized as to expose village men and women to recommendations periodically over time and in such ways that the programme elements reinforce each other. Programme organization is thus seen as a very important consideration in the process of rural development.

There are two major criteria for effective organization of rural development programmes. The first of these is continuity. Continuity refers to the provision in a programme for important recommendations to recur frequently, thus giving people an opportunity to come into contact with important

SUGGESTED GUIDE FOR DEVELOPING AND STARTING A VILLAGE OR BLOCK PROGRAMME
(Useful for specialized segments or for more comprehensive programmes)

Description of the situation: Include only significant facts necessary to clarify conditions for each subject area. Include facts about (1) the people, (2) physical conditions, (3) farm and home practices followed, (4) trends and outlook	*Significant needs:* Using facts about the situation, list conditions in each subject area that show important gaps between what is and what should be. These gaps represent the needs.	*Objectives to be achieved:* Select from column 2 those needs that are agreed upon by the planning group and state them here in the form of objectives.	*Means for achieving the objectives*: Select and list here the primary means of attaining each objective stated in column 3.	*Calendar of work:* Decide and enter in this column the amount of time to be devoted to each major activity listed in column 4, and the dates on which the activity will be performed.
1.	2.	3.	4.	5.

ideas again and again over a time, and, if possible, at advanced levels. Continuity in programmes is basic to the achievement of cumulative effects. It is often referred to as follow-up.

For example, meetings of village people are often held with a little or no particular follow-up on important ideas or recommendations presented. Under these conditions little actual change in people's behaviour has to be expected. Research related to the adoption rate of new practices by rural people shows quite clearly that as the number of exposures to any idea is increased up to five or six, the number of people making changes increases. Provision for the continuity or recurrence of ideas and recommendations several times and over a period of time is, therefore, a highly important criterion that should guide the organization of programmes.

A second important criterion useful in guiding the organization of rural development programmes is integration. Integration relates to the horizontal relationship of various elements in a programme. It has to do with the relationship of one item with another. Programme organization should be such that it helps rural people increasingly to gain a unified view of major programme elements. To be successful, participants in programmes of rural development must eventually recognize all the elements as a whole, and how each one relates to others and to their problems.

For example, the objective of developing an understanding of the value and need for village latrines should also convey the idea of cleanliness and order throughout the village. The idea of integration implies the concept of transfer of learning. It recognizes that people should eventually see ideas, needs and action in relation to the total task of Community Development. Integration implies the opposite of developing ideas singly as isolated behaviours or activities to be applied only at a single place, in a given time, in certain forms. The total capacity of people for Community Development must eventually be developed. Integration helps the officials and the people to see how one item is related to another and how each one is affected by others. Thus, increased breadth and depth of people's educational development and increased unity in their action in relation to important elements in the programme are made possible.

After considering the two major criteria for organizing programmes, questions arise about an organizing structure. Many structures may be used for organizing programmes. These include specific subjects or projects like animal husbandry, cooperatives, small industry, home science and social education. A second common way of organizing programmes is according to problem areas like health, income, agricultural production, housing, home conveniences and farm equipment. A third used structure for organizing rural development programmes is on the basis of broad fields of content, usually designated as production and marketing, family living, youth development and community services.

A clearly developed structure of programme organization helps to assure proper continuity and integration. It helps one to recognize the kind of activity that fits into a programme and that which seems relatively inappropriate. Those engaged in programme planning to meet people's needs, both officials and non-officials, must think and plan together. It is this kind of action that helps assure programmes that end in unity, rather than in a series of separate sets of knowledge, skills and activity. It is only when each element in programmes reinforce others that they make maximum contribution to Community Development.

Some of the devices for assuring continuity and integration in programmes are carefully stated objectives that are well understood by everyone engaged in programme planning and execution, joint planning between officials and non-officials, especially at the local level, long-term planning, annual plans of work, preparation of programmes in written form, and wide distribution of the written programme among officials and the people who are to participate.

CONCLUSION

The development of programmes that harmonize the local needs as people see them and the national interests, with which a country as a whole must be concerned, is a significant responsibility of local non-officials and officials at each level in the hierarchy of publicly sponsored programmes to promote rural development. Any procedure that takes into account the basic concept of needs and meets a set of criteria that will assure that the programme focuses on the significant needs of the people is a good procedure. The measure of success achieved in free-choice societies by public programmes to promote rural development is in direct ratio to the extent to which the programme is built around people's needs and consequently, is an effective influence in helping meet their needs.

To accomplish these desirable ends effectively requires a carefully structured programme at the village and block level that meets the following criteria:

1. It must focus on the felt needs and interests of the people.
2. It must be developed through joint participation of village leaders and block staff, taking into account recommendations from district, state and Central Government personnel.
3. It must be in line with local as well as state and national needs.
4. It must focus on problems that are most important since it cannot be all things to all people at the same time.
5. It must be flexible, but with a 'backbone' that gives it stability and continuity.
6. It must provide for a system of priorities in line with local needs, interests and resources.
7. It must be balanced, that is, contain items of assistance for all major social, economic, age and sex status groups.
8. It must have objectives that are attainable within the economic, social and mental capacities of the people through education with a minimum of government aid.

9. It must be highly significant economically, socially, aesthetically or morally to a relatively large number of people in each village or block.
10. It must be developed, understood, conducted and judged as an educational instrument for helping people learn how to help themselves.
11. It must provide satisfaction for the people who participate. The central objective of India's National Extension Service programme is to help each individual, each family and each village achieve the highest level of living that is capable of economically, socially, and culturally by means of aided self-help through education. Those responsible for developing a programme to achieve this objective must ferret out and perpetuate only the useful from the past, exercise concern only for the promising in the present and focus skillfully all available resources on the significant elements in the bright future. This is the formula for achieving the new India.

SELECTED REFERENCES

- *Approach to Community Development*, Editor Phillips Ruopp, W. Van Hoeve Ltd., The Hague, 1953.
- *Community Development in India,* V.T. Krishnamachari, Publications Division, Govt. of India, New Delhi, 1958.
- *Cooperative Extension Work,* L.D. Kelsey and C.C. Hearne, Comstock Publishing Associates, Ithaca, New York, 1949.
- *First Five-Year Plan,* Planning Commission, Govt. of India, New Delhi, 1951.
- *Guide to Community Development,* Ministry of Community Development and Cooperation, Govt. of India, New Delhi, 1957.
- *Human Problems in Technological Change,* Editor Edward H. Spicer, Russel Sage Foundation, New York, 1952.
- *India's Changing Villages,* S.C. Dube, Routledge and Kegan Paul Ltd., London, 1958.
- *Methods and Programme Planning in Rural Extension,* J.M.A. Penders, H. Veenman and Zenen, Wageningen, The Netherlands, 1956.

- *Pilot Project in India,* Albert Mayer and Associates, University of California Press, 1958.
- *Rural Social Systems,* Loomis and Allen, Prentice Hall Inc., New York, 1950.
- *Second Five Year Plan,* Planning Commission, Govt. of India, New Delhi, 1956.
- *Seminar Papers,* Department of Economics, University of Madras, Madras, 1956-57.
- *What Man May Be – The Human Side of Science,* George Russell Harrison, William Morrow & Co., New York, 1956.

[**Source**: Adopted with grateful thanks from J. Paul Leagans, Extension Education, Publications Division, New Delhi, 1960.]

CHAPTER 9

Each Village as a Unit of Development

When we think of improving the conditions of living in respect to the Dalits in the country we may have to treat each Dalit residential area settlement as a specific unit of development. While we focus especially on the Dalit residential settlement, we cannot ignore the neighbouring settlement more often comprising several caste segments. While we attempt to improve the living conditions of the Dalits, it cannot be an exclusive focus on the Dalit's community though it is the objective, the development agencies may have to consider and involve the neighbouring so called higher caste groups which may in the beginning and over a period of time in the process of development of the Dalits may stand as a barrier sometimes impregnable.

Here we may mention that for centuries together different caste groups have lived in their inherited area assumed close circles of life in terms of values adhered to and acted upon and a kind of distance they maintain *vis-à-vis* especially with the Dalit communities.

It is not simply suggesting or advocating a kind of a sensitive strategy in promoting development of the Dalits. You cannot expect the wholehearted, positive, enthusiastic support from higher caste groups in the neighbourhood, the support for ameliorating the living conditions of the Dalits.

This kind of an operation for development which may take years together is not an easy task. But the approach should be methodical, technical taking into consideration the value system that prevails over millennia in the context of Indian Society.

In the process of this programme there is a need on the part of the developments and change agents to appraise, enlighten and secure the positive support from the higher caste groups in the neighbourhood of the Dalit's settlement.

Though as stated earlier, the focus is on the poor, but it is not possible to totally isolate from the relatively better off people in the various approaches and measures suggested here. These measures relate to the total community. In a limited sense, as a kind of analogy if it rains, it rains for everyone. Poor as the target, some of the measures and efforts made by the administration will benefit the entire community. Keeping in view this object some of the discussions in the work assume a general character. We do discuss the situation in detail in respect of the poor.

The process of organizing rural communities for their participation in development involves working and interacting with the people in the communities. The prerequisite for effective interaction with the people in the rural communities is a knowledge of the characteristics of the rural communities, their way of life, the value systems, traditions and customs, the network or relationships and the kind of changes taking place among them. In the clinical approach, there is a need to consider each village as a unit of development. In order to do this we should have a comprehensive and detailed data pertaining to the village. This will help us in identifying the historical background of the settlement, its natural resources, the kind of avocations people are engaged in, the kind of infrastructure, the topographical details and the human resources the community is endowed with. Further, we may also look into the community common needs and in some cases individual needs also. Treating each village community as a unit of development is a necessity in carrying out gradual sustained development activities in each village. In this context, we may briefly look into the characteristics of the rural communities as a kind of background to understand the general nature of rural communities in India.

Rural communities are not identical in every respect. There is a considerable diversity among them. They could be ranged along a continuum. At one end, we have the sacred-folk societies and at the other end the secular ones, varying in terms of simplicity and complexity. In folk-sacred societies, established practices and ideas are taken for granted. There are few contacts with persons outside of the local geographic areas. Kinship relations are dominant. There is little formalized education; teaching is by means of family training, conversation, preaching and ceremonial. Occupations are learned by apprenticeship. The older men, who have lived longest and whose experiences and memories reach back farthest, are respected and relied upon for advice and guidance. Such societies are relatively changeless; they, in fact, quite generally resist change.

In a highly secular society, means and methods of communication and transportation are ample and ready. Persons are highly mobile both physically and mentally. Formal education is universal occupations and professions are learned as technical sciences. Most social relations are impersonal. Even kinship relations are loose in terms of duties and obligations. Changes of all kinds are prevalent, rapid, and generally welcome. Individuals are members of many groups and live by a number of different value systems.

To be completely bound by folk customs and traditions would mean stagnation. To be completely secular would be inhuman or non-social. No present day society is completely either of them. Those which are nearer the folk end of this continuum are working, some rapidly, toward the secular end of the continuum. The results of too rapid a movement in this direction have been discovered by the study of the most mobile part of the people who live in large cities. The results of little or no movement in this direction are illustrated in a number of countries where a thin layer of wealthy, educated, elite at the top of the social and political structure purposely sabotage change in the large folk segments of their society.

CONCEPT OF COMMUNITIES

Territorial boundary and the sentimental bindings are the essential factors in a community. The group of people that live within a geographic region have the uniformity or similarity in many customs and habits, such as food, clothing, occupation etc. These matters depend upon the availability of material, climatic conditions, nature of soil, etc. The above factors bind the people together.

Another factor, which is the outcome of face-to-face, intensive functional interaction, is the community sentiment. This sentiment that makes them feel that they are one, or the "we" feeling is the life of the community. The sentiment gives rise to responsibility, makes the members of the communities conscious of their rights and duties. Rights and obligations implicate inter-dependence of the members.

A community then means a group of people living in a given area with common interests, bound by a sense of and common mode of living. A village satisfies the requisite to form a community. It gives the inhabitants a common area of land, common past that brings about a sharing of experience and standard of behaviour and attitudes. They share some degree of common activities or some degree of common life, irrespective of their social and religious differences. It is not confined to any of the various restricted fields of community life on the basis of religion, caste, race, language or profession but one that envelops the whole life of the total community. Whatever affects the villages, affects the whole population. A community may be settled or an unsettled one. It may be migratory having come from another area in search of livelihood or it may belong to the new village where they live for centuries, or they might be newcomers.

Some of the distinguishing features of rural community are:

1. Occupation is mainly agriculture and/ or allied professions.
2. People live closer together and closer to the natural environment. This makes their life and attitude simpler and unaffected.
3. Smallness of the size of the community brings the members closer together in everyday life. This and

the common occupational interest make the people know each other better than the urban people do.

4. Lesser density of population is caused by the nature of occupation. People in the rural areas can move more freely.
5. There is greater homogeneity of life than in urban areas; because the people are bound not only by common occupation, but also are bound by common traditions, customs and common heritage.
6. Relatively, there is very little social mobility in the community. They live in the same land generation after generation, by the same occupation, follow the same old customs and habits and maintain the purity of their ethnic identity by avoiding inter-caste and communal marriage or any other type of social intercourse.

Hundreds of local communities in folk societies have been studied by anthropologists. Based on these studies, the characteristics of communities of folk societies can be broadly generalized as follows:

1. Each community is something approximating a complete society in terms of both geography and people.
2. No external forces other than the physical environment enter the community. Few strangers ever come to the community.
3. Each community is composed of families and other kinship groups, the systematic relations between which constitute the social structure of the community.
4. The rights and duties of these groups are passed down from generation to generation and maintained by a value system which consists of the mores of the community. They are accepted by everyone.
5. There are no written constitutions or contracts. Relations between groups are monitored and even enforced by the elders of the group.

6. The community perpetuates itself by teaching each on-coming generations its old way of doing and thinking. Apprenticeship in occupations and initiation into each age group by various types of ceremonial guarantees that each new generation shall know and do as the old generation did.

7. The natural resources with which the people used to sustain their economic life are generally owned by the whole community. Each family sustains itself economically by participating in the development and utilization of these resources, and participates in the economic returns from the resources.

8. The economic relations of the community are the accepted division of labour between groups rather than by trade or even by barter. The economic and social security of all is, therefore, a total community responsibility.

9. There is thus less possibility of change in the status of groups, much less of individuals in the community.

To the degree that simple communities manifest these characteristics, they are whole societies, in terms not only of social, economic and political structures, but in terms of value systems. Each person growing up in one of these communities believes and practices these values, plays his assigned roles without questioning, and as a person is pretty much a complete reflection of the community as a whole.

In the present societies some new types of behaviour develop, but by no means do all the old characteristics of folk society disappear. The total or relative social and cultural isolation of the peasant communities is on the decline. The outside world has moved in on them. Due to multiple factors of influence such as, planned and guided community development efforts on the part of the government, increase in transport and communication, the gradual process of urbanization and industrialization, the emergence of new political and economic institutions, the rural communities in general are in the process of change and the situation in the past few decades may be summarized as follows:

1. The first thing was that trade and commerce entered the village.
2. As contact with trade centers, either with merchants located in the village or with trade towns, developed, at least on the part of a few of the village people there, a knowledge of the outside world in terms of activities about which they had previously known very little. What they learned naturally became matters of gossip within the village and, therefore, some understanding of marketing , prices, and things of that kind developed on the part of all village people.
3. Government had entered all of these villages many years back, but modern government of the type which brings services and assistance to villagers was fairly new in all of the villages. Agents of the government had come in and promoted development and welfare activities. When this once began there was a new basis for forming new parties, and often new factions developed.
4. Government servants, located in or serving the village were seldom local villagers themselves, therefore, new persons, generally persons with more education and receiving higher incomes than the villagers, introduced a new type of person and, in some ways, tended to introduce new social status among the other statuses of the village.
5. Government made incursions in all cases, sooner or later, in terms of establishing and helping to maintain schools. School teachers were new citizens of the community and in some cases, played quite different roles than any outsider ever played in the village.
6. As some youth of the village received considerable education, they became capable of making contacts and did make contact outside the village and thus became a channel of cultural traffic in and out of the village.
7. In a few cases, persons with a degree of education took up new occupations different from those which

they had traditionally followed, and moved away from the village. This has led to occupational and territorial mobility.

8. As the price and market economy entered the village, some persons began making more money. Those who had made more money or had better contacts with outside agencies became money-lenders. Some of them began purchasing land previously owned by peasants who now lost the ownership of their land. Thus a whole new elite developed in the village, sometimes quite a powerful group.
9. In the case of contacts with the market town or with outside sources of income, some of the villages began to attend picture shows and other recreational events outside the village.
10. A new kind of formal and informal leaders emerged. The youth or the younger generation began influencing the developmental activities in the village. In some cases, government servants began to be looked up to rather than feared.
11. In most villages a degree of individualism developed. Some persons were paid special attention by the development agencies. They gained new importance and they tended to form a group which protected the group against the large owners.
12. In most villages, the lower classes, that is, the lower income people, were paid special attention by the development agencies. They gained new importance and they tended to form a group which protected the group against the large owners.
13. It may be stated here, that the same old reverence for elders, and for the set class structure, and even for the villagers' values, had been considerably diluted.

The rural communities are, however, far from having lost all their old folk characteristics. The following such characteristics, though somewhat modified, are still maintained.

(a). The elders, while they no longer constitute the village government, are highly respected and are still counselors in many types of issue.

(b). The village community's organization is perpetuated by each new generation tending to follow the family occupations of previous generations.

(c). There is in all of the villages some division of labour between the families, this division being fixed by the traditions of the community.

(d). Families, generally extended families, are more integral social groups than are the villages as a whole.

(e). Sentiment for the land, pride and tenacity in the ownership of the land, is still very strong.

(f). There is relatively little tolerance for new ways of thinking and doing. If the people were asked to choose between tradition and progress, tradition would perhaps be their instinctive choice although a second choice might induce them to take a few hesitating steps in the direction of change.

REFERENCE

Taylor, Carl (n.d), *Community Mobilization for Group Formulation*.

CHAPTER 10

Local Institutions as Primary Agents of Social Change

People's participation in the sense of sharing their ideas, interests, needs and views with the development agencies could be direct and indirect. Direct people's participation in any development activity is constrained, besides other community factors like its size, its geographical spread, and in other words the population in the community and its social composition. One logical, practical and simple mechanism for people's participation is institutional representative participation wherein people's elected, selected, nominated representatives, of diverse people's bodies (organizations/ institutions) from the village to national level participate on behalf of people and for expressing their views. These are formal statutory bodies like village panchayats (India, Nepal), Tambon Committees, Mandals, Samithis, Unions (Thailand and India) and Upazillas in Bangladesh (suspended after General Ershad's exit) and Zilla Parishads in India. Apart from the above statutory bodies which are the administrative and institutional products of decentralization we may also cite voluntary and feeder organizations such as Youth Clubs, Women's Clubs, Farmer's Forums and all forms of cooperative societies facilitating institutional representative participation of the people in the promotional and developmental activities.

Decentralization at the district and sub-district level in terms of policy formulation, planning, resource mobilization, allocation of resources and implementing development programmes is a measure and a means to bring down development administration close to the people for their active involvement. Democratic decentralization is a facilitating factor in representative people's participation and this takes us to look into the various facets and dimensions of decentralization.

DECENTRALIZATION: ISSUES, EXPERIENCE AND POLICIES

Decentralization means decreasing the role of central government, and augmenting the authority of responsive local institutions. It is concerned with increasing accountability between people who provide local services, and the people who use these services. Above all, it is about the improved management of some of the development activities in the rural area. There are many forms that decentralization can take, including transfer of authority from central to local government, from provincial government to community and non-governmental organizations, and to the private sector. It is a tool for better rural management, by changing the institutional framework to include a significantly greater role for local and community institutions. Decentralization is official policy in many countries of the region. It is no longer an issue whether local governments will assume greater responsibility, but how they will perform the functions statutorily devolved and entrusted to them.

Whether the formal or constitutional structure of the state is federal or unitary, governmental functions are performed in most countries at several levels. While responsibilities for some of the crucial functions such as defence, external relations and macro-management of the economy rests with the national government, several other functional and technical services in agriculture, education, health care and social welfare are usually the responsibility of the administration at the sub-national or local levels. In some Asian countries, the administrative structure is made up of more than two tiers, with the second tier looking after subjects like law and order and justice, and the planning and execution of development programmes at the regional or provincial level, while government bodies below them are entrusted with the responsibility for providing basic civic services. In developing countries, although forces favouring centralization have usually been strong, a common tenet of policy has been to decentralize governmental functions and foster the growth of local government.

It is universally acknowledged that certain functions of the state are best performed at the local level for the simple reason that decentralizing the provision of basic civic services (eg. Sanitation, public health, primary education and social welfare activities) maximizes welfare by responding efficiently to public needs. Local governments responsible to the people from the locality are in a better position to respond to the preferences and needs of the people than governments functioning at a distance. To a developmentalist the decentralization of the powers and functions of the government among different levels, which essentially underlies the rationale for federalism, helps to reconcile the aims of achieving unity in the midst of diversity. From the economic point, optimal provision of public goods calls for both centralized and decentralized decision-making in the appropriation and allocation of resources in the public enterprises.

In the developmental context, decentralization acquires special significance in view of the fact, given the requisite authority, local bodies can generate activities suited to the resource endowment and needs of the local people. Local government units can undertake more effectively activities like improving local infrastructure, such as roads, transport and communication facilities, water supply, electricity and energy, apart from delivering social services in the area of health, nutrition, sanitation, housing, and so on. Local governments can also make valuable contributions to irrigation and land utilization, the protection of the environment, animal husbandry, household industry, public works and the supply of inputs for agriculture and cottage industries. Excessive centralization in planning and implementation of development programmes often causes needless delays and wastage while stifling local initiative. It is increasingly recognized that real grassroots development can take place only with the active participation of local government bodies in these activities.

Local units are also perceived to be in a position to tap resources, which centrally administered revenue, instruments cannot reach. Participation of the people in the government at the local levels makes it possible to tap resources in ways which may not be acceptable if imposed from above.

The healthy growth of local government units together with the representation of the people also helps inculcate participatory government and development. The units can serve as a training ground for the people and their representatives in responsible decision-making and meaningful participation in national life. Above all, it helps to impart a sense of fulfillment among the people as citizens and thereby strengthens the foundations of a democratic polity. These considerations, as well as the widening resource gap of the public sector in many developing countries, which underscores the urgency of developing more resources and ensuring their efficient use, have impelled many governments to look to decentralization as a partial answer to their problems.

Despite recognition of its merits, however, and the resolve to decentralize governmental functions in planning and management, the process of decentralization is yet to strike roots in most developing countries. Planning has to be decentralized if idle resources are to be utilized optimally and local needs and aspirations are to be met efficiently. Diseconomies and other costs of over-centralization coupled with advances in technologies, particularly in the field of information and telecommunications, have made decentralization both imperative and feasible.

The term "decentralization" in the context of governmental organization is generally taken to mean the transfer of authority from the national or central government to its field offices, local authorities or other local bodies. Decentralization in the economic sense implies the transfer of responsibility for planning, management, resource raising and allocation of resources in the public sector. Such resource transfers can be effected through the devolution of powers and functions of government to lower-level bodies with a degree of autonomy, by the deconcentration of central government offices, and by deregulation, and with the setting up of public enterprises.

If the benefits of local participation and involvement in deciding the use of national resources for public purposes according to local preference are to be derived, decentralization has to aim at what is implied by "devolution". Such devolution should proceed to the lowest possible level where the people can effectively participate in development and have direct access to the benefits of growth as well as civic and social services that governments provide to their citizens. It follows that to be meaningful, devolution carries with it the need for introducing an element of self-governance or some representative character in the lower-level government bodies to whom responsibility for specified functions, along with requisite powers and autonomy, is transferred. Fiscal decentralization, which essentially implies a greater access to national resources with increased powers to mobilize and use them for meeting local wants, provides the real content of functional decentralization.

While decentralization has been attempted in developing countries in all the forms distinguished above, the picture that emerges from the close scrutiny of the countries shows that progress in devolution has been rather slow and halting. Seldom was the intention to devolve matched by necessary action, and even where action was taken in the form of legislation or creation of necessary institutions, other conditions for devolution to be effective were not met with. While there are more than two tiers of government in all the countries, few have succeeded in devising local government institutions which could involve the people in the function of government and in its various activities. At this point, we may at length look into, in a larger sense, a revolutionary change in India – democratic decentralization and Panchayati Raj.

PANCHAYATI RAJ

The institution of Village Panchayat is as old as Indian history and is part of Indian tradition. The ancient Panchayats discharged most of the functions affecting the life of village communities and were effective units of administration until the eighteenth century. With the advent of the British, however, they got relegated to subservient place in the colonial administrative set-up. Even during the British rule, particularly after Ripon Resolution of 1892, attempts were made to revive these village institutions. Accordingly, Panchayats and Local Boards were set up in the Provinces of British India.

The Need for Panchayati Raj: The Constitutional Sanction Behind It

The Panchayats, the Taluk and District Boards and the Municipalities established after Ripon, were either purely nominated or containing some members elected by narrow electorates. Under Montague-Chelmsford Reforms, Local Self-government was made a transferred subject and the State Ministries concerned attempted to broaden the foundations of these local bodies.

In some States, Village Panchayats were sought to be established on a wider scale. But all these efforts were half-hearted and the establishment of Village Panchayats and reconstruction of other local bodies on a truly democratic basis figured prominently on the platform of the Indian national Congress.

After Independence, the importance of revitalizing the Village Panchayats and assigning them a specific role in administration was recognized and it was laid in the Indian Constitution as a Directive Principle of State Policy that "the State shall take steps to organize village Panchayats and to endow them with such powers and authority as may be necessary to enable them to function as units of Local Self-Government" (Article 40).

Its Relevance to Community Development in India

The first organized effort to tackle the problems of rural India was through the Community Development Programme, which was launched in fifty-five selected projects on October 2, 1952. The programme, based on an integrated approach to the various aspects of rural development, emphasized from the beginning the importance of working through the people's institutions like Village Panchayats, Cooperatives etc. to ensure their involvement in the planning and implementation of development programmes and to secure the fullest possible public participation. A great deal of consultation and development work was done under the National Extension Service Schemes. The Planning and Development Committee set up in each Block was merely advisory.

After the Community Development Programme, which was gradually expanding to cover larger areas, was under implementation for about four years, in January 1957, a Study Team under the Chairmanship of Balwantray Mehta was appointed by the Planning Commission to review the working of the Community Development Programme and also to examine the question of reorganization of district administration to provide for popular organizations between the Village and State levels.

The Study Team recommended, *inter alia,* the setting up of elected and organically linked democratic bodies at the village, block and the district levels and the entrustment of all planning and developmental activities to these bodies. This recommendation was accepted by the National Development Council in 1958. The Central Council of Local Self-Government in its fifth meeting at Hyderabad in 1959, took stock of the action taken by the States to implement the decision of the National Development Council and recommended that "while the broad pattern and the fundamentals may be uniform, there should not be any rigidity in the pattern. In fact, the country is so large and Panchayati Raj (democratic decentralization) is so complex a subject with far reaching consequences, that there is the fullest scope of trying out various patterns and alternatives. What is most important is the genuine transfer of power to the people. If this is ensured, form and pattern may necessarily vary according to conditions prevailing in different States".

All States have accordingly undertaken to establish Panchayati Raj. Thus we find the ideology and the objectives of Community Development and the concept of Democratic Decentralization-building or extending democracy to the grassroots are fused together, and christened as "Panchayati

Raj". The new statutory institutions have become the agencies of Community Development Extension Programmes. In essence, this was further growth in the previous programme designed to strengthen the people's own democratic, elected organization by opening new avenues of opportunities for their development. This new device offers the villagers a share in their own direction and self-development which is indeed a new and a novel departure in their lives. In this programme the people under their own organizations at the Village, Mandal, Block and District level were given equal share and status in the working of the whole community development block. Village Panchayats are constituted through elections and given democratic powers and responsibilities. The Sarpanchs or the Presidents of all the Panchayats formed a Panchayat Samithi, the Panchayats formed a Samithi at the block level and Samithis constituted the Zilla Parishad at the district level. The functions of the Rural Development Agency and the people's organizations at all levels up to the district are to further strengthen and make the rural development programme more dynamic and its structure more complex.

"The Community Development approach has to be an essentially democratic approach as this will draw large masses of the people as active partners in the tasks of developing the vast country. For, only thus can this gigantic task be accomplished. The Community Development approach, while it will depend on the democratic process, will at the same time also help to strengthen it. There is, therefore, complete inter-relationship between Community Development and the progress of democracy; they are two sides of the same coin. Both are processes of human development. It is for this reason that the Community Development Programme came to focus attention on the importance and urgency of democratic decentralization. Democratic Decentralization must not be understood as merely the creation of Local Self-Governing Institutions of the people at different levels or as transfer of real power to the people. Its object is to give vitality to the whole democratic process and to provide to a new born democracy a wider and firmer base" (Mukerji, 1961).

BASIC ELEMENTS OF PANCHAYATI RAJ

The term "Panchayati Raj", which is popularly used in the country includes the two words Panchayati and Raj. Panchayati means "of the Panchayat", which consists of a group of "Panchas" who are representative leaders of people at the village level. What is emphasized is the representativeness of Panch, irrespective of how this element of representativeness is determined. The word "Raj" in this context means Government. The term "Panchayati Raj" therefore, literally means "Government of People's representative leaders". In this sense it is an expression of the essence of democracy as internationally understood. The Balwantray Mehta Committee Report expresses this categorically in these words: "in the ultimate analysis, the establishment of the Panchayat Samithis with a wide devolution of powers by the State Government has to be an act of faith-faith in democracy".

The fundamental or basic principles of Panchayati Raj emphasized in the COPP Report are:

(a) It should be a three-tier structure of Local Self-Governing bodies from the village to the district, the bodies being organically linked up.

(b) There should be genuine transfer of power and responsibility to them.

(c) Adequate resources should be transferred to the new bodies to enable them to discharge these responsibilities.

(d) All development programmes at these levels should be channeled through these bodies.

(e) The system evolved should be such as will facilitate further devolution and dispersal of power and responsibilities in the future.

The primary objective of Panchayati Raj is to establish an integrated structure of local democratic or self-governing bodies linking the village within the district and to make the Village Panchayat as a unit of planning and execution of all schemes of rural development. Secondly, Panchayati Raj aims at developing the initiative of the local people and create conditions for maximum popular participation. Thirdly, it seeks to develop sound leadership at all levels in the district necessary for the success of democratic institutions. And finally, it seeks to provide at the instance of Panchayati Raj bodies, a development-oriented and efficient administration.

In terms of organization or structure, the programme of Panchayati Raj, as mentioned earlier, envisages three tiers of the Government from the village up to the district level. These three tiers are:

1. Panchayat at the village level consisting of elected representatives of the people with provision for the co-option of two women members and one member each from the Scheduled Castes and Scheduled Tribes.
2. At the Mandal or block level, an elected Self-Governing Institution to be called Mandal Parishad Panchayat or Samithi. Membership in this to be by indirect elections from the Village Panchayats. Its jurisdiction to be coextensive with a Mandal or Community Development Block.
3. At the district level there is a body called Zilla Parishad. In order to ensure necessary co-ordination between the Mandal Parishad or Panchayat Samithis, Zilla Parishad was constituted which consists of the presidents of the Mandal Parishads or Samithis, and elected political representatives of the area namely MLAs, MPs and district level government officials.

In recent years there has been changes in the size, nomenclature and mode of election to the above bodies one example is Andhra Pradesh.

Three tiers viz., Village Panchayat, Panchayat Samithi and Zilla Parishad when constituted and operated simultaneously make up the structure of Panchayati Raj in a district. Functionally, Panchayati Raj is assumed to be operative to the degree that it results in the community understanding its problem, realizing its responsibility, exercising the necessary powers through its chosen representatives and maintaining a constant and intelligent vigilance on local administration.

PROGRESS OF PANCHAYATI RAJ

Panchayati Raj, as mentioned earlier, is an institutional arrangement for decentralized planning and plan implementation. It was brought in to enhance and facilitate people's participation, even though it was representative type of participation. Panchayati Raj was first introduced in Rajasthan and Andhra Pradesh in 1959. This was on the recommendations of Balwantray Mehta Committee on Plan Projects (COPP) appointed in 1957. This was followed by the Ashok Mehta Committee in 1978 which made vital suggestions for restructuring the Panchayati Raj bodies. It recommended three-tier system of Panchayati Raj institutions and direct elections to Chairpersons of all the three tiers. It also recommended election of women to Zilla Parishads and the Mandal Panchayats, and in case no women were elected to these bodies, they are to be co-opted. Ashok Mehta was followed by three Committees i.e., G.V.K. Rao (1985), L.M. Singhvi (1986) and Bommai (1989). Amongst other recommendations of these Committees was reservation of seats for women in these bodies to a tune of around one-third.

Though the spirit and objectives of democratic decentralization are the same in all the States in India, there are a few variations in terms of number of tiers, their structure, nomenclatures, levels of their operations and provision in them for women representation. The lowest tier is called Gram Panchayat, the middle tier is variously known as Panchayat Samithi, Panchayat union and Mandal Parishad, and the tier at the district level predominantly goes as Zilla Parishad and in a couple of cases as District Council. The idea here is only to indicate the institutional structure and not to go into the details of their constitution and mode of elections, co-options and ex-officio membership at the middle and the upper tiers.

As of December 1992, the following States have a three-tier structure of the Panchayati Raj system: Andhra Pradesh, Bihar, Gujarat, Himachal Pradesh, Karnataka, Madhya Pradesh, Maharashtra, Orissa, Punjab and West Bengal. In case of Haryana, Kerala and Tamil Nadu, it is of two-tier structure at the village panchayat levels and block levels which were earlier community development blocks.

TOWARDS FUNCTIONAL DEMOCRACY

Panchayati Raj is in our making. Statutory changes alone do not bring in the desired changes and transform the human elements. Slowly, patiently, and methodically the statute must be translated into action. For a planned social change towards a richer and meaningful life for the masses in the countryside, an inter-disciplinary approach is the means. A scientific approach to the problem is the answer. Hit and miss methods may not pay higher dividends in the long run. Panchayati Raj must become more a way of life of the rural people.

In a democracy the individual is no more than a spectator; he is actually one of the spectators. He cannot play his part unless he is properly informed as to the processes of democratic government at all levels. Planned public relations are essential to inculcate civic spirit, civic pride and civic unity in villages, as the percentage of literacy is low, a judicious selection of the media of public relations will have to be made. The radio, the film, civic exhibitions, civic weeks and civic *melas* are some of the useful tools of public relations in rural area. Civics with due emphasis on rural self-governments should be made a subject in the curriculum of schools, colleges and universities.

In a greater measure, the people's representatives are to deliver the goods. On them depend the development of the local community the strengthening of the democratic institutions and largely the success of the Panchayati Raj. This development of local leadership and responsible and responsive citizenry could be achieved only through Social Education Programmes apart from economic measures. The community must be mobilized, interest groups identified and organized into responsive and dynamic groups. This mobilization of the community into institutions, interest groups and associate agencies will create the conditions necessary for the emergence of leadership at the local level.

It is only by educating the general public, could we expect awareness, leadership and initiative among the elected members of the Panchayat or of higher tiers, we cannot neglect the general mass and merely concentrate on the elected representatives. A massive adult education movement is desirable to educate the general mass. Literacy Programmes should find a predominant place in the adult education movement. All illiterates below 40 years must be made functional literates within reasonable time. Further, radio-forums and reading rooms-cum-libraries could be organized for dissemination of knowledge.

It is needless to emphasize that the elected representatives should be trained and educated in all aspects of Panchayati Raj. In the course of the Panchayat term, the Panches (or the sarpanches and up-sarpanches as the case may be) should be trained at least twice-once soon after their election to the office and for the second time, in the middle of the term. The stress must be on utilizing the institutional facilities available and not on merely creating institutions.

In educating the sarpanches and the panches the Extension Personnel in the Community Development and more especially the Extension Officers, panchayats could play an effective role. At least once in a quarter or six months, the Executive Officer of the Panchayats may convene a meeting of all the sarpaches and panches of one or two gram sevaks circles at a convenient place and arrange for talks by special invitees – officials and non-officials on Panchayati Raj. This may help understanding and motivating initiative on the part of the elected representatives.

There is no element of force or coercion in making people do things. The means are constant persuasion and education.

Multitudinal problems arise in the working of the Panchayati Raj Institutions. These problems need scientific treatment and solutions arrived at on empirical studies. Action research with an interdisciplinary approach to the problems is a must in the field of planned social change. Under such a built-in action research programme the social scientists and the administrators have to devise ways and means to ensure effective and active participation of the elected representatives in the working of the Panchayati Raj.

An attentive study of the process of decentralization in various countries suggests a few impeding factors in decentralization.

ABSENCE OF LEGAL FRAMEWORK

The disappointing progress of efforts to decentralize can be attributed to a lack of adequate constitutional and legal backing and a weak fiscal base that is fundamental to such a process. We may say that India is an exception in this kind of lacunae. In many instances, local bodies have failed to come up with legal support provided through constitutional recognition or separate legislation. This is true irrespective of whether the country in question is federal or unitary. In Pakistan, a federation, several attempts were made in the last forty years at the initiative of the central government to set up local governments throughout but none has been of much avail. In Thailand, a unitary country, the local level bodies with elected assemblies have been created through specific legislation laying down the structure as well as the powers and functions of the local bodies at different levels. Local governments are, however, not in a position to perform more than a few functions assigned to them by the laws which brought them into being (Cohen and Uphoff, 1977).

LACK OF FISCAL AUTONOMY

A more serious impediment to the functioning of local autonomy is the financial dependence of the local bodies on the central and provincial governments. Almost invariably, the bulk of the financial needs of local governments are met out of the share of the national taxes, and / or subsidies from the center or grants, and the dependence seems to be increasing.

The domination and control of local bodies by the central and provincial governments, which is partly attributable to their financial dependence, has also been responsible for stifling local autonomy and blocking decentralization. In most cases the central government is unitary type and the central and provincial governments in federal structures exercise control over the local bodies in various ways, direct and indirect. In Thailand, while the degree of control varies between different local bodies, all are subject to close control by the central government. Central control is maintained in Thailand through a system that allows the Ministry of Interior directly to control the administration of all local bodies in the kingdom. Supervisory powers over local bodies are delegated to the provincial governors, who are also assigned responsibilities to monitor the activities of local governments. The statutory authority of the local bodies to raise certain taxes and incur expenditure is subject to the rules and regulations of the central government.

China is perhaps the only country to have seen substantial decentralization. Although a country with "unified leadership and government", China has in practice allowed considerable latitude to the local government entities, the provinces and the municipalities, in their function. Even though the country has a unified national budget, the provinces and municipalities have their own separate budgets and run enterprises often on a large scale. Decentralization gathered momentum in the 1980s and in fact the pace appears to have been too rapid for the country to adjust. It may, however, be fair to say that much of the freedom which the local governments enjoy in China despite a monolithic political structure stems from their relatively strong financial base (Cohen and Uphoff, 1977).

FISCAL MISMANAGEMENT

In country after country what has prompted higher level interference is financial mismanagement. In Thailand, the financial weakness of the local bodies is attributable partly to the inefficiencies of the local governments themselves and their inability (or unwillingness) to make full use of whatever tax powers they have under the law. The poor yield of the house and building tax which constitutes the most important component of local taxation in Thailand is due both to deficiencies in the structure of the tax as well as inefficiencies in its administration. While liberal exemptions undermine its base, administrative inefficiencies have also stood in the way of its effective implementation and tackling evasion practiced in various ways by landlords. Tax rolls and maps are not updated and cadastral maps of even resourceful local authorities like the Bangkok Metropolitan Administration are

40 to 60 years old. The system of billing and maintaining tax rolls is outdated. According to a recent estimate, computerization and regularization of the tax-payers would alone double the yield of the tax. While with urbanization one would expect a rise in the revenue from this tax, its contribution to local revenue has gone down (Jurgen, *et.al;* 1989).

ADMINISTRATIVE WEAKNESS

In many countries, especially at the district and municipal or village levels, there is lack of trained manpower to levy taxes efficiently and mange their affairs. The elected officials or representatives furthermore do not always display the sense of responsibility or dedication required for fulfilling the objectives of the local government and often engage in intrigues for power, seeking personal gain to the detriment of public interest. Super-session of local bodies in several countries has also often followed from their mismanagement and the failure of the democratic system to work at the local level (Cohen and Uphoff, 1977; Jurgen, *et al.;* 1989).

STRATEGY OF PLANNING FOR DEVELOPMENT AND EFFICIENCY ARGUMENTS

An important factor impeding the process of decentralization in the developing countries is the adoption of planning as a strategy of development with considerable involvement of the public sector. A degree of centralization is inherent in a strategy of planning, with the government taking a lead role and laying down the basic programmes and priorities at the national level to ensure consistency and efficiency although decentralization might lead to faster development of better-endowed but less developed areas, central intervention and allocation of resources were often thought necessary to bring about the balanced development and provision of public services at a minimum level in all parts of a country. Modern technology with the vast economies of scale spilling across regions in areas like power and communications also have reinforced the trend towards centralization. A lack of expertise in and familiarity with modern techniques of harnessing and managing natural resources also have strengthened the case for a certain degree of centralization. In addition, there are the gaps in technology, resources and skills at the local levels which cannot be made up without help from above. The creation of specialized agencies or authorities to undertake specific tasks like metropolitan planning and development is often motivated by considerations like these.

Considerations of efficiency also argue for centralizing certain important functions, as do the centralized collection of the major taxes like the income tax, which unavoidably created a vertical fiscal imbalance in the system and so the dependence of the local bodies on higher level governments. This is compounded by their lack of managerial and technical skills. Denuding the central government of its command over resources also undermines its capacity to even out regional imbalance, as is now being witnessed in China.

RECENT TRENDS

Experience of the last three decades has, however, cast doubt on the efficacy of centralized planning in promoting growth and spreading the benefits to all sections. Moreover, disenchantment with over-centralization has led to a search for other ways of decentralization apart from devolution. Given the will, it is argued, solutions can be found for the problems and dilemmas or at least these can be rendered manageable. Although decentralization often gets stalled because of a lack of managerial skills, there are examples of good results achieved by associating the people in governmental activities at the lower levels. The involvement of the local population in some of the States in India where elections to panchayats were held in recent years seems to have activated hitherto untapped energies and resources and made tangible contributions to improving public services and activities in those regions. There have been several instances of positive gains from the association of local people and organizations like village cooperatives in the past in Thailand, Pakistan, India and Malaysia. Besides, not all the weaknesses of the local bodies of their own making. As already mentioned, their fiscal powers are often constrained by central control exercised in various forms.

As is to be expected, decentralization, even when acknowledged as desirable, encounters resistance from those for whom it implies a loss of governmental power and authority. A striking example of how the central authorities tend to shackle the autonomy and initiative of local bodies, even when the involvement of local government is sought, is provided by the guidelines issued to district councils in India to implement an employment programme in the rural areas in the late 1980s. Rodinelli and others conclude their discussion on what impedes decentralization with the following observations:

"Untimely however, decentralization is an ideological principle, associated with objectives of self-reliance, democratic decision-making, popular participation in government, and accountability of public officials to citizens. It is a political decision, and its implementation is a reflection of a country's political process and maturity". (Rondinelli *et.al.,* 1983).

These observations are equally valid even after a decade and a half. The recent experiences and trend show that there is now greater political awareness of the need for decentralization than before. Hence, the search for solutions to the problems encountered in its implementation and the urge to draw lessons from the past.

Decentralization with its full complements of vertical geographic devolution of powers, administrative control, financial and resource raising authority, freedom of allocation of resources and mandate and responsibility to development planning and plan implementation at local levels, by itself is a great leap forward in the governance of public interest and welfare. People's and people's representative leaders' participation in all the above functions will strengthen the roots of democracy and ensure enduring people-oriented development.

REFERENCES

Cohen, J M and Uphoff N.T, (1977). Rural Development Programmes: Concepts and Measure for Project Designing: Implementation and Evaluation. Rural Development Monograph Series No.2; Cornell University, USA.

- Jurgen, Ronald (1989). Local Governments in South East Asia. HSD Working Paper, Asian Institute of Technology, Bangkok (Thailand).
- Mukherji, B. (1961). Community Development in India, Orient-Longmans, New Delhi.
- Rondinelli, D., *et al.*, (1983).Decentralization and Development. UNCRD Regional Development Series, Japan.

CHAPTER 11

Local Leaders, their Role and Participation in Alleviating Poverty

There is a close relationship between the leadership in a rural community and the nature and degree of their participation in rural development activities. The local leaders may be instrumental in mobilizing and motivating people to participate in development activities or they may sometimes be barriers inhibiting and subtly or deliberately discouraging participation for their selfish ends and or do so out of ignorance, misinformation, avarice, or trying to keep their followers as marginal and occasional beneficiaries of development programmes and not as active participants in decision-making or authors of any policy issues.

Participation in development programmes as a product or function depends on the structure and type of leadership and the ethnic, social and class composition of the rural community. Sometimes, the numerical strength of the ethnic, occupational and professional groups are factors to be reckoned with when we speak of local leaders as stimulants or barriers to people's participation in development programmes.

We may have a brief look at the rural leadership and some instances wherein local leadership was a deciding factor for any initiative for promotional or developmental programme or the local people accepting a project, innovation or participating in a communal activity.

The village community world over, despite its social, ethnic, religious and lingual composition, is a social entity. It has its structure and traditions. The diverse activities of the community, both individual and communal are carried on and regulated by some individuals from within and outside the community. The individuals who guide, who are sought after to guide and shoulder the affairs of the people in the village may be called leaders. Sometimes, the pattern of leadership and its functions vary from community to community. It is interesting to look into the principles that control human relations and how a social group organizes and lives its life. More often, the burden of village responsibility rests on the leaders just as family responsibility rests on the head of the household.

AREAS OF LEADERSHIP

Leaders emerge and function in diverse fields. The areas of leadership and the number of leadership and the number of leaders functioning in each area and one leader functioning in several areas depend on the size and social structure of the rural community and, as mentioned earlier, on the occupations and profession of the population, their literacy and intellectual levels, and also on the degree of their interaction with the outside world.

In a broad sense, when we think of rural-traditional communities, the following activities may be considered as areas wherein the question of guidance and consulting arise and the local leadership centre around these functions.

1. Coordination of village communal undertakings.
2. Liaison between the people and governmental personnel.
3. Guidance in times of epidemics.
4. Guidance in religious magical matters.
5. Financial problems – monetary matters.
6. Political matters.
7. Guidance in legal matters.
8. Financial help for marriage and death ceremonies.

9. Settling quarrels-disputes outside the village.
10. Settling quarrels-disputes inside the village.
11. Agricultural matters.
12. Guidance in educational matters.
13. Guidance in warding off the effects of witchery and sorcery.
14. Guidance in employment opportunities.

As communities progress, with the increase in skills and literacy rate and change in the value system the nature of needs, degree of dependency and also leadership change. Leadership is a social phenomenon and it is subject to change and will in some measure, in some areas persist forever.

LEADERS AS FACILITATORS AND BLOCKERS

One comes across innumerable instances in rural communities and equally in urban settlements too wherein local leaders function as motivators and facilitators encouraging and enthusing people to participate in development activities concerning their community and as blockers discouraging the people in participation. The local leaders have been instrumental in accomplishing several projects for their communities. Participation by significant individuals in the community secures the projects as a sanctity, approval and acceptance by the generality of the community. We may look into a few cases wherein the weight and significance of local leaders manifest itself.

PARTICIPATION FOR A NATIONAL CAUSE

During the Indo-China War in the last quarter of 1962, over the border dispute which lasted for a short period, the Government of India had to mobilize its resources and a fund raising campaign was started all over the country. It was called "War Fund". The State Governments were asked to raise funds from the people and they acted through several of their line and development agencies. During this period what were then called Community Development Blocks were given each a certain target of amount to be raised from People's Contributions towards the War Fund. As usual (we mean the target distribution downward in the hierarchy) the Block Development Officer (BDO) assigned each Village Level Worker (VLW) a certain target of amount to be raised in his circle comprising households ranging from 1,500 to 1,800.

During this period the author happened to be a VLW and the target of raising money for the War Fund fell on him. Inclusive of hamlets he had around twenty villages under his jurisdiction. Indo-China war was a distant cry for the people in the area. Many of the villagers had no idea of China, its geographic location and its borders with India and the disputed borders. It became a big problem to explain the situation to the simple but intelligent villagers. We had to approach the local leaders for help in raising the amount. Through the initiative taken by the local leaders, we were able to raise small amounts of money ranging from one to twenty rupees or so, from each household.

In this context the author would like to cite one instance pertaining to a community of shepherds in one village, most of them poor and landless, mainly thriving on rearing sheep and goats. We told them that the millionaire-farmer and politically influential leader of a higher caste community from the neighbouring village was visiting their village on such and such a day and he expected them to contribute their mite for the War Fund.

The day the leader visited the shepherd community, one could see the spontaneous and enthusiastic presenting of old silver bangles, rings, waist-strings made of silver, the only valuable ornaments some of the families possessed. Most of them had no money to give. Some of the silver ornaments given by them can be considered antics, for they were of old-fashioned and some may be called of tribal-wear. Later, we sold the silver ornaments to some well-to-do families and passed on the proceeds to the BDO. The participation of the people in this instance was overwhelming and largely it was to be attributed to the respect the villagers had for the leader and his very visit to them seeking their humble contribution. As mentioned earlier, to a large measure, the people's response and their contribution, as a symbol of their participation for a national cause was not a response to Government nor to those skirmishes taking places at the international border between India and China, but for the influence and initiative of the local, small leaders and the big wealthy leader from the neighbouring village.

The following two cases reflect the spirit of healthy competition amongst the rural communities and the significant and appreciable role-played by both, by the formal and small informal leaders in effecting popular participation in mobilizing resources to start a high school and forming of approach roads to the villages.

Small Informal Leaders Collecting Contributions from the Villagers for a Large Educational Project

Rampur is a fairly big village with a population of around three thousand at the time of this incidence and is located in Chittoor district, Andhra Pradesh, South India. It is a multi-caste community. It is a market center for the main villages and hamlets within a radius of 15 km. The population of the cluster of villages around Rampur in 1960s was around 30,000, but there was no high school in the whole area. The majority of the population comprised small farmers, landless labourers, artisans and petty traders. Since there was no high school within the walkable distance and many families could not afford sending their children to distantly located high schools and keep them in hostels, many children had no chance of going beyond primary education.

As a contrast to the conditions of the commonality of the communities under reference, one family of the dominant caste-Hindus in Rampur was rich. This family and its clanfolk and kin in the neighbouring couple of villages and other districts were traditionally affluent. The head of the rich family in Rampur is a graduate, well-informed, with high connections, wielding influence with the administration at the district and at the State level too. He is a big farmer, moneylender and most of the farmers in the neighbouring villages were to borrow money from him and so they were captive sellers of their groundnut produce to him only. He was politically powerful and whether the people like it or not he had a sway over them and there was no opposition to him. He could send his children to expensive public schools and colleges and so he had no felt-need for a high school in the village. The neighbouring villagers felt an acute need for a high school in their area. It was reported that some of the important people in the area approached this rich man and raised the question of a high school for the area. His response was evasive, with excuses and explanations of impracticability of opening a high school in the village to serve the village and the neighbouring communities. A high school was a long felt-need. The neighbouring villagers sensed and realized that the big man was not interested in a high school in his area, may be thinking that if the children of poor families received higher education, his importance and his family status will go down, when poor get educated and become rich it is a threat to the already rich.

A few leaders in the neighbouring villages took initiative, went around the villages, discussed with local leaders the prospect of raising money from each family after the harvest of paddy and groundnut, the principal crops in the area. This silent campaign for raising contributions was done without the knowledge and approval of the big man of Rampur. It was a successful fund raising campaign. Obviously, the message of popular concerted efforts, mobilization of small resources in cash and kind and the community's solid social action reached the big man as a shock and threat to his eminent position. He realized that he could not stall the starting of a high school for the area, for the people were determined, have raised considerable amount from the people to approach the government for sanctioning for opening a high school in their area. They were to offer their collections as a matching contribution to government's grant. The big man realized that it was already too late and even if he opposed subtly or diplomatically the opening of the educational institution, it would come with the popular force. And so, not to be left behind and sidetracked he sent invitation for a grand feast to all-important leaders in the neighbouring villages. Some of the invitees knew that it was a face saving mechanism. A large group gathered on his spacious mango garden and after treating them with a rich feast, he gave a small speech, how, for a long time, he had been pondering over the need for a high school for their area and that he was glad that some initiative was taken by the local leaders and the people in the area and announced with a flourish that he was donating three acres of prime land close to the main road in his village for the high school and certain amount in thousands and wished that the high school may be named after his late father.

After a few months the high school was sanctioned by the government. From then on the big man assumed the lead position. The buildings came up. The high school was opened and for the past forty years now the children of this area have access to higher education. It is the small informal and formal leaders in the rural communities, who initiated the movement and secured popular participation. We should acknowledge the help rendered and boost given by the big man in Rampur whatever might have been his initial attitude and intentions for a high school to serve the needs of the common people in the area.

PARTICIPATION IS CONTAGIOUS

When an occasion arises, when proper climate is created, when people's competitive spirit is kindled, when people perceive the tangible benefit for them and when properly guided by the local leaders people's participation in promotional and development activities becomes contagious. The term "contagious" is used here in the sense of exciting enthusiasm from one to the other for a positive course of action.

It was Andhra Pradesh in India which was the first State to introduce Panchayati Raj system in September 1958, in the Community Development Blocks that were in operation during this period. In order to celebrate the first anniversary of the Panchayati Raj system in the State, a grand programme of multiple development activities viz., kitchen gardens, soak pits, drainage, mass environmental sanitation and formation of earthen approach roads to the villages where they did not exist then was initiated. Of all the above programmes, the formation of cartable and suitable approach roads to villages was given the place of primacy.

The present case refers to the former Chowdepalle Community Development Block in Chittoor district, Andhra Pradesh. The approach road campaign in particular was carried on for a couple of weeks by the Community Development Workers and local leaders. Prizes were established for the best people's participation in terms of their labour contribution in forming the roads. For a few weeks it looked like a massive festive activity in dozens of villages, people engaged in cutting, digging, forming and aligning the earthen approach roads to their villages. One could see the spontaneity and enthusiasm among the people. It was really contagious. Later, the VLW circles which had the best performance were selected and the concerned Village Level Workers were awarded the prizes by the Block Agency. Here the credit goes to the people and their leaders.

WHAT HAPPENS WHEN A LEADER IS IGNORED?

As mentioned earlier in this chapter, participation by significant individuals in the community secures the projects of a sanctity approval and a legitimacy. The local leaders are the gate keepers and one can visualize the role of these gate keepers in rural communities. We may look into the case wherein an educational institute as a development agency failed to contact a local leader and solicit his involvement in a housing project for the cobbler community, a constituent of the village. The failure to contact the leader by the development agency was not deliberate or negligence, but it was out of ignorance of the personnel of the development agency, and local communal dynamics and the leader's influence over the cobblers. The non-involvement of the local leaders of different caste and religion acted as a stalemate to the project in the beginning.

SERVAIPURAM

Servaipuram is one of the villages in what is called Achampatti complex of villages, close to Dindigal town in Tamil Nadu. The complex comprises around ten villages which used to be the service area of Gandhigram Rural Institute. The institute had several extension and service activities such as pre-school education, women's clubs, agricultural societies (for access to credit), leather tanning and housing for the weaker sections. The institute was receiving funds from a German voluntary agency and this was the only source of funds for the institute for its extension service activities. These activities served as a field orientation to the students of the institute.

Servaipuram is fairly a large village with a population of 2,500 persons. The majority comprised of Servai Christians and there is a church in the village with a priest who was an outsider and a local leader as the manager of the church. Obviously, the manager of the church was a Christian and was religious and secular leader in the village. Nothing in the village should happen outside his knowledge. He had a grip over the Hindu minority groups in the village.

THE COBBLERS

One such minority group was cobblers, the leather workers comprising 45 households. All these families were living in hovel like huts, crowded in a small area outside the main settlement of Servaipuram. The most immediate need for the cobbler community was housing. The institute's faculty (the author was one of the faculty) on deliberations with the cobbler community arrived at this priority of housing for them. The housing project required acquiring of land for house sites and building the houses for the 45 families. The leaders in the cobbler community were asked to choose some land around the village (private or government land) so that preparations may be made for formal acquisition of land for housing.

The faculty from the institute used to meet the cobblers periodically in order to know the progress in their selection of land. Thus, the faculty spent ten months without getting any indication from the cobblers. Whenever the faculty assembled the cobbler leaders and discussed the question of their choice of house-site, the response was silence or some vague and evasive answers. The faculty was at a loss as to why the cobblers were not coming forward with any indication of their choice of land for their new houses. After ten months of futile meetings with this clientele group, the faculty at one point asked them as to what was holding them in making a decision. The leader of the cobblers came out in an hesitant way and in a faltered tone informed the faculty that they better consult the manager of the local church. Later, it surfaced that the manager of the church felt that he was not consulted by the institute's faculty and he was ignored though he was also a secular leader of all segments in Servaipuram. He had kept vigilance on what was going on between the cobblers and the service agency. It came to be known that he mildly and indirectly warned the cobblers that he was not happy about what was going on between the cobblers and the service agency. The cobbler leader threw a hint at the faculty that better they discussed the house site affair with the manager. The faculty realized the lapse on their part that they have failed and did not bother to know the nexus of relationship between the cobblers and the majority Servai Christian community and more importantly the influence of the church manager. He blocked the activity, since he felt that his importance was not recognized and the programme did not go through him.

After a few days this lapse was remedied. The faculty went to the manager, apologized for having been ignorant of his status and his importance as a local leader and arranged a big meeting of the community including the cobblers and the manager was requested to preside over the meeting wherein the housing for the cobblers and other programmes (a community hall, loans for draught bullocks, a kindergarten) were discussed. Later on, the housing project for the cobblers was routed through the manager. We cite this case in order to emphasize as to what happens to development programmes in rural communities, when individuals do not participate in the development activities.

Further, it is not only a question of enthusing, motivating the existing local leaders to encourage and induce participation among the people, but it is also cultivating new leadership in the local communities to generate and institutionalize more and more of people's participation in development activities. Activities or programmes are the means to build new leadership and strengthen the existing leadership. Local leadership is an invaluable human resource and energy to build up healthy rural communities on the plank of participation.

CHAPTER 12

Role of Youth in Alleviating Poverty

Youth constitute a potential and a rich human resource in any community. The youth with the vigour of their age, most often bubbling with enthusiasm for change for better ways of life look for opportunities to fulfill their psychic, social and economic needs. It depends on how the youth is motivated, mobilized, organized, facilitated and utilized in building newer and progressive communities. The programmes should satisfy them and should also be contributory to community development.

When we speak of the rural youth, we meet with a diversity in their case, literate, illiterate, people with some social and technical skills, rich and poor, employed and unemployed. And so the rural development programmes are to be satisfying and challenging to them so that we can secure and ensure their participation. The youth are involved in development programmes as adults in general and there are special schemes like the National Service Scheme (NSS) in India wherein the students of colleges and universities, volunteer and contribute their labour in forming approach roads, digging irrigation canals, and other kinds of manual work beneficial to rural communities.

Youth development or involvement of the youth in development forms a department in the ministry of Education, Human Resources Development in some countries (e.g., India) or a separate ministry as in the case of Bangladesh. We may focus on twin objectives in this chapter-developing the youth and the youth developing the family and the community which may be called "Family-based Integrated Youth Development".

FAMILY-BASED INTEGRATED YOUTH DEVELOPMENT

Developing the youth is of prime importance in all societies. Ministries of Youth Development and in some cases the Departments of Youth Development have been attempting the development of youth in creative, constructive and productive activities. But it has been realized that by focusing on youth alone, the desired kind of development changes among the youth are not encouraging and commensurate with the efforts made. It is found necessary that youth development should be an integral part of family and community development. At least in the initial stages, there is a need for an intensive coordinated approach and effort in developing the youth and their families simultaneously- the youth contributing to the parents and the family and the parents and the larger community guiding, helping and giving moral and socio-economic support to the youth and involving them in constructive and productive activities.

Such a desirable youth-family development could be achieved only through a systematic approach which may be termed as "Family-based Integrated Youth Development".

OBJECTIVES

The main objective of family-based integrated youth development is to take each family as a unit of development, study its material and human resources and help the members in the family in their developmental pursuits and assist them in utilizing their physical, material and human resources for increased productive activities. In other words, in the programme, we look at each family, take stock of what its resources are, how the resources are utilized today, how best they could be utilized, the kind of support they need, develop initiative and motivation among the youth and the adults in the family in order that they mobilize their own resources. In addition, technical and managerial guidance and marginal monetary assistance is extended to them so that each family attempts a maximum level of resource utilization, physical as well as human.

PROGRAMME CONTENT

In the proposed scheme, the activities will comprise moral, spiritual, social and economic programmes for the youth for their own progress and for the betterment of their families and their communities. The on-going programmes in the Ministry or Department of Youth Development will be carried out intensively involving each family as a unit of development.

Basically the scheme will comprise social and economic components. The emphasis in the scheme is maximal utilization of the internal resources of the family and the community, mobilizing the youth as instruments of change.

The programme may comprise:

1. Collection and processing of family-community data.
2. Identification of small enterprises, self-employment avenues which may be taken up by the youth and their families.
3. Preparation of feasibility studies on small enterprises.
4. Training of the youth to take to small entrepreneurial activities.
5. Organizing the youth into viable associations.
6. Involvement of the youth in community development activities.

COVERAGE OF THE PILOT SCHEME

In view of the clinical-family community-intensive integrated youth development, initially as a pilot measure two units each comprising 5-8 villages may be taken up under the pilot scheme. Preferably one pilot project may be selected in a better off area and another in a backward region. The two pilot project schemes will lend themselves for comparison and future replication of the programme. The criteria for selecting the pilot project areas may comprise:

(a) The cluster of villages or the blocks/unions selected for the pilot project are neither too close to an urban center nor too isolated.

(b) The units selected currently carry on satisfactory youth development activities and have the response and immediate potential for intensive development; and

(c) The units enjoy minimum transport and communication facilities and some infrastructure for small enterprise development.

INSTITUTIONAL ARRANGEMENTS

The existing organizational set-up of the Ministry or Department of Youth Development at the district level may be utilized for planning and implementing the programme in the pilot area with a small staff to keep in touch with and monitor the youth and a small staff to keep in touch with and monitor the youth and family development activities. A small information-monitoring center in each village of the pilot area may be established which will have in its office the family resource and development cards pertaining to all the families in the communities. In addition to the youth development agency, the other promotional agencies may be involved in planning and implementing the activities. The data and information system will be maintained at the pilot project headquarters concerning all the villages in the area. It can be envisaged that each family will have a "Family-Resource and Development Card". This card will contain basic data about the family; its members, their age, educational attainment, how they are occupied, means of livelihood, how their present assets are utilized, their income and expenditure, their needs, the way they would like to improve their conditions and potential and scope for further development with external guidance and assistance. The data from the family cards will be aggregated both at the community level and pilot project level. The data could be classified in different ways both at the village and the project levels for purposes of planning and implementation of programme.

ORGANIZATIONAL SETUP

The overall functioning and administration of the pilot project will be under a "pilot project committee" comprising elected or nominated youth representatives from each village in the pilot project area. There may be one or two representatives from each village and wherever there is response women also may serve on the committee. The committee will elect a chairman from amongst themselves to head the committee.

The committee will be entrusted with powers to decide, formulate, implement and monitor all activities under the"Family-based Integrated Youth Development". The committee will be assisted by an executive wing consisting of an executive officer and field and secretarial staff. The executive officer may be the Assistant Director of Department of Youth Development or any officer with a different title but with a similar function. He will guide and assist the committee in its deliberations and decision-making. It is envisaged that the pilot project committee and the executive wing are complementary to each other and they are to work in unison.

Staff of the Pilot Project

1. *Project Executive Officer:* He will be in overall charge of the project.
2. *Rural Social Analyst:* A qualified person in social sciences with experience in social surveys and human resource development. He will be responsible in assisting data collection, processing of data etc.
3. *Field Investigators (two):* They will assist the Rural Social Analyst and most importantly the youth volunteer investigators who will collect data pertaining to families and the community.
4. A Secretarial Assistant: A steno-typist-cum-cashier.
5. An Office Attendant.

It is envisaged that the secretarial and transport assistance will be provided by the Department of Youth Development.

APPROACH TO THE IMPLEMENTATION OF PILOT PROJECT

To begin with, detailed data as mentioned above, in respect of each family will be collected by the youth in the community as volunteers with the assistance of the project officials. The *Family resource and Development Card* will be so designed that it will contain basic data about the family and also will have provision to record subsequent development activities etc. A copy of this *Family Resource and Development Card* as mentioned earlier will be with each family and one at the village center and another at the project headquarters. At any given time it is possible for the family, community and project to know the present position and what is happening and what should be done at three levels; family, community and project. A monitoring system of to and from informal dissemination will be developed, sometimes using computer facilities where necessary. The *Family Resource and Development Card* will serve as a reminder and as a progress card of the youth and family developmental activities. It involves initial information gathering and recording of the data and coding the families, the activities and the communities in the project area. In the monitoring system, there will be regular and periodical feed-back and evaluation in respect of each family and community. In the total process of planning, implementing and evaluating the activities, the youth will be the principal participants.

TIME FRAME

The first cycle of the two pilot projects will have a two-year period. During this period the basic data of the families and the community will be prepared and aggregated at the community and project levels. Programmes of action will be formulated. Youth organization and other institutional arrangements will be made. Programmes of immediate and long-range activities will be planned and scheduled for implementation.

The pilot scheme suggested above could be extended to all the rural areas depending on the success gained in the pilot schemes and with improvements too. The youth involved in the programme could be those educated, high school dropouts looking for employment or self-employment and those who are still doing their studies in secondary schools and colleges. The objective is to benefit the youth and at the same time make them active participants in rural development.

CHAPTER 13

Sanitation: A Critical Factor for Development

"The causes for the bad sanitary conditions in the villages are physical, economic, socio-cultural and psychological."

The sanitation in most of the villages in India presents a dismal picture. It has been a perennial problem, so complex in its character posing a threat to public health. The situation deserves utmost attention and consideration of every individual, local institutions, corporate bodies and the Government at large, for it affects our health and living.

The Japanese are said to be meticulous in their personal and environmental cleanliness. They take as much care of the precincts of their dwellings as they do in the case of their drawing room and bedroom. After a picnic party is over, the Americans do take pretty care to see that they do not leave any litter behind. They leave the place as clean as it was before. What an appreciable civic sense it is! And what do we do here? And what is the environmental sanitary condition in the Indian village?

By sanitary environment we mean a place or village where the residential quarters, cattle sheds, the village precincts, lanes and streets, are regularly swept and kept clean, free from open ditches, pools or slushes, dungheaps or garbage and faecal matter fouling the whole surroundings. A clean village is one free from the above and enjoying drainage facilities and arrangements for regular disposal of refuse. But today most villages in India present a dismal picture. Indiscriminately deposited dung and garbage heaps in various stages of decomposition, ditches and unwanted dirty water pools, ugly looking lanes and streets are some of the characteristic features of the villages. The insanitary conditions pose a constant threat to public health, being the root causes of innumerable diseases and spread of epidemics.

THE MULTIPLE CAUSES

The causes for the bad sanitary conditions in the villages are physical, economic, socio-cultural and psychological. In regard to the patterns of settlement of Indian villages, there are mainly three types – the dispersed or scattered type, the nucleated or the cluster type and linear type i.e., houses built on either side of a road in rows. The nucleated or the cluster type poses many sanitary problems in regard to space for drinking water wells, drainage, bathing and lavatory facilities, disposal of refuse and for sinking of soakage pits. Many of the villages were unplanned houses clustered together with narrow lanes or no lanes at all. Some ancient villages are walled around as a measure of protection from wild animals and thieves. And there will be fields around the village narrowing down the residential quarters. Where the houses are congested and where the villages are situated in low-lying areas, drainage is a problem. So, the very pattern of village settlements, the narrowness and physical or spatial limitations on the expansion of some villages, the topographical features of villages lead to bad sanitary conditions.

In a broad sense, occupation or economic activities of the people also decide the type of environment they live in. India is predominantly an agricultural country. Agriculture in India means use of cattle for draft, milk and manurial purposes which mean housing the cattle in separate sheds and the collection and depositing of dung and other waste materials. Lack of improved cattle-sheds and sheep-pens is a problem in the villages. Either as a matter of convenience or due to socio-cultural and religious attitude of the villagers, the cattle sheds are located near the living quarters and there may not be any wall separating the living quarters and the cattle shed. In many cases the cattle dung and urine are not properly collected. The droppings of cattle, sheep, goats and of poultry strewn all over are usually not taken care of. Even though each household attends to its own immediate surroundings, the village lanes and streets are nobody's responsibility. The villagers also dump indiscriminately cattle dung and all waste material of considerable manurial value around the house and the immediate surroundings of the village. This is due to congestion of space, feeling of difficulty in carrying the matter over a long distance to the fields or outskirts of the village. The indiscriminately dumped dungheaps are seldom covered as a measure to conserve the nitrogenous content in the matter or to prevent foul or stinking smell emanating from them.

Lack of drainage facilities in the villages and the habit of open defecation on the part of the villagers are other common causes for disgusting sanitary conditions. The open defecation is a psycho-cultural problem. The villagers are used to it. A change in this habit is long overdue. Either the villagers could use sanitary type of latrines or the centuries old habit of open defaecation persists. The simple fact is that over 90 per cent of the villagers were not used to a flushout latrine in their lives.

Illiteracy, poverty and lack of contact with the outside world contribute to the low civic sense among the villagers.

Another source of insanitation is the drinking water well that lacks raised platforms and causes cesspools making the place dirty.

THE BLEAK BACKGROUND

Illiteracy, poverty and lack of contact with the outside world contribute to the low civic sense among the villagers. Further, the places where shandies and weekly markets are held, when not maintained properly, add to the insanitation of the area. Chewing and indiscriminate spitting is another common social phenomenon.

Having been used to a bad sanitary environment, the villagers do not shudder at anything dirty. The tendency is to take things easy.

There are over 5,80,000 villages in India – just one village per two square miles over the surface of this sub-continent. Now all the villages in India come under the village Panchayat administration. The Panchayats vary in geographical, topographical and economic conditions and cultural practices. Each area in view of its diversity needs a special treatment to solve the problem of environmental sanitation.

In the case of those panchayats which have adequate income, water facilities and have a permanent establishment for sweeping and scavenging, the question of village sanitation is not serious. But the problem becomes acute only with the minor panchayats which cannot or do not have sweeping and other facilities, nor do the villagers in such panachayat areas attend to general sanitation of the village.

Thus we find small villages suffering from (or enduring) a distressing and disease-producing sanitation. Most villagers are aware of the problem, but a remedy is beyond them.

Rural sanitation finds a prominent place of importance in Gandhiji's constructive programme. He often emphasised the magnitude and importance of village sanitation. He practised what he preached. He himself swept the streets and cleaned the latrines. He introduced the ***wardha*** latrine (trench type) which is beneficial in two ways – preservation of night soil (for manurial purposes) and preventing the fouling of village surroundings through indiscriminate defecation.

LOW PRIORITY

Civil amenities and environmental sanitation are statutory functions of the village panchayat. But apparently the order of priority goes to items like water supply and street lighting and mostly sanitation is not accorded the importance it deserves.

Programmes to improve rural sanitation find a place in the Five Year Plans. Individual and mass sanitary drives were targeted items in the community development extension programmes. These drives in the initial stages were effective and successful and attained a great degree of publicity. The villagers and the school children participated in the drive enthusiastically. Local leaders, officials, men, women and children held brooms in their hands and cleaned the streets. In this, an attempt was made to drive home the dignity of labour and to create among the villagers a new awareness as to the prime importance of the upkeep of the village.

Civil amenities and environmental sanitation are statutory functions of the village panchayat. But apparently the order of priority goes to items like water supply and street lighting and mostly sanitation is not accorded the importance it deserves.

Allied to the sanitation programme are the propagation of sanitary type of latrines, sinking of soakage pits where there are no drainage facilities, construction of *kacha or pucca* drains, improved cattle yards, urinal trenches, scientific methods of compost making, provision of refuse bins, pavement of lanes and streets. This integrated approach is aimed at promoting sanitary conditions in the villages.

Some of the officially sponsored programmes could not make any headway. There were certain inherent shortcomings. Strictly speaking there was no scientific approach on the part of the extension and public health personnel in introducing innovations. The rural workers dictated by a conceptual frame of modern sanitary amenities and accessories as provided by the agencies tried to implant new ideas and habits in the rural communities. For instance, the construction of public lavatories (flushout latrines) in the villages at a considerable public cost was a thorough failure. First, there was no sufficient involvement and commitment of the villagers in this programme. There was the problem of water scarcity. While we discuss the question of rural sanitation water should not be treated as an isolated factor. Above all, the failure in the use of the public latrines was mainly due to the villager's attitude and habits. An attitudinal change is what is desired.

The second factor is limited governmental allocations for programmes connected with village sanitation. Thirdly, poor and inadequate finances of the panchayts and lastly the general apathy of the villagers towards sanitary measures.

As observed earlier, rural sanitation is a complex problem warranting a perspective plan and short-range specific measures to promote better sanitary conditions. The rural

Development Agency, the village panchayat, the village school and the voluntary organizations such as youth clubs and mahila mandals could play a significant role in this respect.

The supply of technique, personnel and funds depends on the Government. The programmes towards better sanitary conditions in the villages should be flexible enough so that they could be modified in accordance with the local conditions. A survey of attitudes, felt-needs and specific problems of the villagers should precede on scientific lines before the programmes are formulated. In introducing innovations, the approach should be scientific and institutional. The techniques of group-involvement, group-commitment, propaganda, publicity, demonstration, etc., must be made use of. In other words, the extension methods must be fully employed so as to motivate the villager to use a sanitary latrine and keep the precincts of his house clean. This is a slow, painstaking process. It must be gone through. There is no short cut to it.

In each rural area the vulnerable areas of insanitation and the factors causing unclean conditions are to be located, studied and remedied. The dungheaps should be taken care of. If the villagers are educated on scientific lines of compost making, the ever exposed heaps will not foul the village with stinking odour and become a breeding source for flies and insects. Wherever possible a common compost yard a little away from the village could be established. This could be done by the village panchayat. Drainage depends mainly on two things – the physical feasibility of constructing drains and financial resources. Wherever these two are positive, depending on the size of the village, *kucha or pucca* drains could be constructed as a phased programme. Areas where either of the two is absent, soakage pits are better substitutes. It falls to the lot of the individual householder. Sinking of soakage-pits is cheap and is within the capacity of the commonest man in any village. The only limitations in digging soakage pits are availability of space within the housesite and the composition of the ground soil in the house site. In case of loose soil the soakage pit is not to be located close to the draw-well because of percolation of impure or contaminated water from the soakage pit to the draw-well.

Strictly speaking, the panchayat is responsible for ensuring better sanitary conditions in the panchayat area. In the budgetary allocations of the panchayat enough provision must be made for water supply, drainage, public latrines and refuse bins and recurring expenditure towards sweeping, scavenging, etc. Every panchayat has its annual and Five Year Plans. The panchayats which could not afford full-time sweepers for daily sweeping of the village, could at least appoint either a less number of full-time or more number of part-time sweepers, in order that the villages are kept clean at lest once a week. It is desirable that this minimum programme is carried out by every panchayat.

In regard to the using of sanitary type of latrines by each family, the panchayat should take the initiative and lead in their introduction not only as a civic measure but as a persuasive step creating facilities and favourable public opinion in the use of latrines. In achieving the above-mentioned ends the panchayat can enlist the cooperation of the village school, youth club and mahila mandal and work in unison with them.

The voluntary organizations in the villages could take up village sanitation as one of their main activities and arrange periodical mass sanitary drives. The mass sanitation drives, if carried out sincerely over a period of time, are bound to influence the general public and change their attitude, make them sane to keep their surroundings clean.

The village school as one of the three basic institutions in the village could take the lead and function as a pioneer and model in sanitation programmes. It could function as an experimental and demonstration centre for a soakage pit, a lavatory, a compost pit and for environmental sanitation. The school children could be very easily trained to make use of a sanitary latrine, providing one at the school. They carry their ideas and habits to their homes and it may result in a flush-out latrine in their homes. Further, under the guidance of the school teacher the children learn the importance of environmental sanitation and could even participate in the periodical mass sanitary drives organized in the villages.

PUBLIC HEALTH CESS

Some of the corporate bodies at present are engaged in rural developmental programmes. It is a welcome sign that they have assumed this role as partners in rural development. Their role in rural uplift will become more significant and pointed if they could concentrate on rural sanitation. They may take up programmes such as provision of drinking water, sanitation which will include drainage, latrines and gobar gas plants. The Government may also consider income tax relief to the corporate bodies in respect of the amount they spend towards rural sanitation. Further, the nationalized and scheduled banks which have adopted some villages for development may lay emphasis on programmes of rural sanitation. The Government may also bring in legislation towards what may be called public cess. The public health cess as a certain percentage of land revenue will go to the village panchayat and the amount will be utilized exclusively for rural sanitation.

Thus, we see the problems of rural sanitation in India today are deep-rooted, complex and important demanding the attention, cooperation and coordination of the Government, statutory bodies, educational institutions, voluntary organizations and above all the understanding of the general public.

CHAPTER 14

Measures to Alleviate Poverty among the Dalits

In contrast to many other developing countries, a comparatively sophisticated redistribution system for the poorer sections of the population was established during the sixties and seventies in India. There are benefit programmes for marginal farmers, rural development programmes, crash schemes for rural employment, intensive rural employment programmes, food for work programmes, programmes for ecologically disadvantaged areas and minimum needs programmes.

If poverty went down during recent years it was probably much more the effect of these deliberate efforts than of economic growth as such. Nevertheless, it is much easier to finance these programmes in a situation of growth. The Indian government has spent 37 billion Rs. on anti-poverty programmes during the sixth plan period (1980-85). This is an impressive amount in absolute terms but it represents little more than 0.5% of the national product during this period. This relative figure is indeed very small if one compares it with unemployment and social security schemes in western industrialized countries. Dandekar has recently calculated that it would cost 98.600 Million Rs. per year to bring all the poor, including the urban poor in the unorganized sector, above the poverty line.

This would constitute one third of the government revenues. Such a programme would drastically change the structure of government outlays but one cannot argue that an antipoverty programme which would wipe out absolute poverty completely in India is inconceivable. A substantial increase in expenditures on antipoverty programmes should be vigorously supported by development assistance. India is now one of those countries which receive very limited amounts of development assistance in per capita terms.

DEGRADATION OF URBAN ENVIRONMENT IS CAUSED BY RURAL POVERTY

As far as sanitation and the provision of clean drinking water are concerned, these tasks are being undertaken through time-bound programmes by State Public Health and Water supply Organizations. However, it is necessary to look beyond the statistics of targets and achievements compiled by these authorities and recognize the fact that sanitary conditions are deteriorating rapidly in almost all towns and cities, primarily because of the continued influx of the rural poor who set up slum colonies and even start living on pavements in search of livelihood. Municipal bodies are finding it increasingly difficult to cater even to the minimum sanitary needs of such immigrants. Open defecation and urination have become familiar sights in and around slums, and constitute a grave threat to public health.

The caste-Hindus have a stake in adding fuel to the fire. They sow the seeds of discord amongst the poor to prevent their uniting, and exploit the underprivileged as landowners, employers, traders and money-lenders. They not only try to nip resistance in the bud, wherever and whenever it occurs, but misuse those programmes designed to improve the lot of the poor for their own benefit. And one of the main reasons for this is that they want to prevent the poor from becoming economically independent of them.

ANIMATION AND FACILITATION THROUGH VOLUNTARY AGENCIES

The poor and underprivileged are hardly in a position to improve their lot on their own, but need impulses provided by well-meaning outsiders. These are people who do not belong to the poor but, for different reasons, want to help them by establishing non-profit organizations. In the past century, in Europe, too, industrial workers, craftsmen pressed hard by industrial enterprises and petty farmers, needed such persons to found cooperatives, trade-unions and labour parties.

The Voluntary agencies (VAs) fulfil usually several tasks, which fall into two categories: animation and facilitation. In reality, one cannot clearly distinguish one from the other. Animation means, first of all, conscientization of the poor. Animators help the poor to regain their self-confidence and self-assertiveness. Only when the poor regard themselves as equal human beings and citizens do they question the reasons behind their poverty, realize their rights, request changes, discover the abilities and capacities at their disposal, have the confidence to change established patterns of behaviour and dare to use their assets to promote their own interests.

Once the poor have been motivated and activated by conscientization, the animator changes into the role of the facilitator. He assists the poor in forming groups, in deciding which measures should be taken and in executing the same.

He acts as their intermediary to get access to governmental or commercial services. He, for example, manages to establish first contacts between the poor and the official banking sector by helping to provide the securities banks require (seed money, incentive deposit, group guarantees), and by helping the banks to change their procedures in such a way that they meet the requirements and abilities of the poor.

VAs provide legal aid to the poor and their groups in their disputes with the rich and the government authorities, they encourage them to unite in federations or to take part in support net-works in order to promote their common interests collectively, and establish themselves as institutions at the service of those of the poor who have no access whatsoever to any services.

Those VAs which are serious about grassroot development are aware that they themselves do not know the direction in which the poor will move. They present themselves, therefore, not as teachers and know-alls, but as equal partners and, by skilful questioning, make them conscious of their problems, prompt them to identify the causes and to propose solutions. VAs should not be hierarchically structured, but need a code of conduct and an organizational form conducive to participation.

Even though there are tens of thousands of VAs in India, many of them are only of local importance, and others do not work as altruistically and efficiently as would be required in the best interest of the poor. And this is the reason why, so far, they could not contribute to a large extent and with a lasting effect towards the eradication of poverty by strengthening the demand system.*

But anti-poverty programmes are probably far more difficult to implement, vastly more expensive and also likely to take time. The land reforms programme, with all its many limitations, belongs to this category. But the effects of the land reforms vary from State to State, depending on the nature of the reforms and the earnestness with which they were implemented. But, by and large, the reforms have removed from the scene holders of concessional tenures such as zamindars, jagirdars amd inamdars and have made it extremely difficult for absentee landowners to keep their land except where they belonged to the dominant castes. The reforms have also benefited tenants and cultivators in some States. Further, special programmes have been devised for two categories of poor peasants, called "small" and "marginal" farmers, which have proved to be helpful, though here again there are differences between States in the seriousness with which the programmes were implemented.

The food-for-work programmes, in areas where they exist, enable landless labourers, the weakest section of the rural population, to find work during the lean agricultural seasons. Some States have modest housing schemes for the weaker sections: The importance of such schemes is often not so much in the quantum of relief provided but in making known to the people that a new order is round the corner. The same may be said of some other programmes such as attempts to provide free lunches for school children, low-interest bank

---

Source: Adopted form the material – Problems of International Cooperation – "viertel jahres berichte" December 1987

loans to the poor to enable them to be self-employed and very modest pensions to poor widows and old men. In this connection, the abolition of the institution of "bonded labour" is important, in as much as this category of agricultural servants have worked very hard and paid very low wages. Informed observers of the rural scene in India think that the institution still survives in the more backward areas and besides, not all emancipated labourers have been rehabilitated. Some State Governments are also actively trying to provide electricity and pure drinking water to villages in backward areas. The total effect of all these innovations has been to instill hope in people who had long suffered neglect. The quality of life in India's villages is beginning – only beginning – to change. And that is a big thing.

But the removal of poverty, stupendous as the task is, is only part of the struggle to control population growth. Further, the initial effects of the removal of poverty may only be to exacerbate the problem. It is time that disincentives were also thought of for promoting family planning, instead of relying entirely on incentives, as is being done so far.

Rural society is hierarchical in more than one sense, though it is usual to refer only to caste while considering hierarchy. But there is also a hierarchy based on the ownership of land and everyone who owns a sizable quantity of land has to become a patron in order to have an assured supply of labour and services. Patrons generally come from the high or dominant castes. When the members of a dominant caste own the bulk of the arable land in the village or local area, then the caste as a whole wields substantial power over the artisan, servicing and labouring castes which supply the clients. Here the point needs to be made that traditionally, that is, in pre-British times, it was not land that was scarce but labour, and a landowner had to look after his labourers reasonably well in order to retain them. But with the enormous rise that has taken place in India's population during the last 150 years, the quantum of arable land has shrunk drastically, and concomitantly, competition has sharpened greatly among clients in order to have access to land. Naturally, this has drastically reduced the ability of the clients to hold their own against exploitative patrons.

The patron-client relationship was traditionally a multi-stranded one, the patron being employer, creditor, arbitrator, and generally, friend, and protector, while the client was bonded labourer, tenant, sharecropper, debtor and general factotum. The client was expected to serve his master loyally, and have his interests at heart and promote them. In rural India, several groups of patrons and clients came together to form a faction, and a village is usually split into two or more factions. While the personnel of factions changes over time, and bits of one faction hive off occasionally to join another, an outside threat frequently leads to the closing up of the factions except when factionalism runs very deep. Factionalism is a part of the rural social structure, like caste.

A patron's clients included the members of the artisan and servicing castes who worked for him, and their families. The clients were paid fixed amounts of grain at harvest. They also had roles in the patron's house at life cycle rituals, and they were paid for this separately.

But a radical transformation is beginning to take place in the relations between patron and client. Clients are now increasingly paid cash, and this is particularly true of the agriculturally prosperous areas. Now infrequently, outside labourers are employed in preference to traditional clients, as they are more hard-working, and cheaper. The rules of noblesse oblige are giving way to the exclusive consideration of profit, to the disadvantage of clients.

This leads us to rural migrations. During the last four decades, agriculturally prosperous regions are attracting labourers from far and near. Labourers from dry or unirrigated areas gravitate to prosperous areas in search of work. In a sense, immigrant labour acts as a depressor of wages, but it is also a source of income to some of the poorest people. In a society without the benefit of state-supported social security schemes, poor immigrants would have gone to the wall but for the new work opportunities available in the rich agricultural regions.

Nowadays, mass migrations occur of seasonal workers from Orissa and Eastern U.P. to Haryana and Punjab. Similarly Marathi speakers in the north-western region of Maharashtra migrate to neighbouring Gujarat for seasonal work. Besides inter-state seasonal migration, there is much intra-state seasonal migration all over India. Such migration is welcomed by landowners who would not be able to transplant, weed or harvest their crops otherwise. But while landowners may welcome immigrant labourers, indigenous labourers do not. Immigrants not only bring down wages but they are also used to "discipline" indigenous labour. Since a good proportion of the latter will be members of the Scheduled Castes, they will be antagonistic both to their high caste employers and to the immigrants. This may lead to conflict between the affected Scheduled Castes and their high caste patrons, or assume the form of a conflict between indigenes and outsiders.

A most depressing scenario for the future is that concerning the relations between dominant, landowning castes and the Scheduled Castes. The conflict between the two is likely to become more and more bitter, and violent. It will be a primary arena for the struggle for equality in India.

Traditionally, as is widely known, the Scheduled Castes performed certain essential tasks in the villages, some of which like sweeping and scavenging, removal of dead animals, and doing leather work, were considered polluting as well as degrading. They were also important as agricultural labourers. They suffered from a number of collective disabilities, and were also obliged to show deference to the higher castes in speech and gesture, failure to do so being punished by the latter.

But the position of the Scheduled Castes is changing, and the pace of change likely to be faster in the near future. Thanks to the policy of protective discrimination, many members of the Scheduled Castes have been to school and college, and are holding white-collar and professional jobs. Some members of the Scheduled Castes have a higher standard of living than many members of the high castes. Again, thanks to reservation, some members of the Scheduled Castes are elected legislators at various levels while a much smaller number have become ministers. Not only do high caste candidates, seeking election to a legislative body, have to approach members of the Scheduled Castes for votes, but many members of the high castes have to approach Scheduled Caste ministers for a variety of favours. And it is well to remember that these events are happening for the first time in the history of India.

But in spite of the changes which are occurring in the relations between the high castes and Scheduled Castes, large numbers of the latter are acutely dissatisfied at what they consider to be the slow pace of change. The young and educated members of the Scheduled Castes are particularly dissatisfied, and angry. Open defiance of the authority of the high castes is encountered increasingly, especially among some groups such as the Mahars in urban Maharashtra. During the early seventies, the Mahar had an organization called the Dalit Panthers, deriving inspiration from the Black Panthers, which was committed to the promotion of the cause of the Scheduled Castes through recourse to violent revolutions The Panthers were responsible for producing a body of protest literature called "Dalit sahitya", rejecting caste, inequality and exploitation. Now "Dalit sahitya" exists in other Indian languages also, contributing to the militancy of the Scheduled Castes and the "weaker sections" generally.

While the Scheduled Castes have made some substantial gains, and as already mentioned, pollution ideas have weakened somewhat, large numbers of people, particularly those in the rural areas, do not accept the idea that the Scheduled Castes are their equals. The progress achieved by some Scheduled Caste members, has only roused the anger and envy of many members of the high castes who attribute the formers' success to the special treatment accorded to them. The refusal of some Scheduled Castes to perform one or other of the many traditional duties imposed on them, is seen by the dominant castes, as an affront to their dignity. They think that the government is pampering the Scheduled Castes, and encouraging them to defy the authority of the higher castes. No wonder then that violent clashes occur frequently between bands of the dominants and the Scheduled Castes: the latter are beaten up, their huts set fire to, and their women raped. Such clashes are not confined to rural areas though they are far more common there. They seem to be more frequent in the Hindi-speaking regions than elsewhere, but the latter areas are not free from such clashes.

It is likely that such clashes will increase in the coming years. As more and more members of the Scheduled Castes get educated and assert themselves, resentment against them is likely to increase. The fact that even in 2006 A.D. about 70 percent of the population is likely to be rural, will mean that India's villages will each become a mini-battlefield for inter-caste conflict. Since resentment at the progress of the Scheduled Castes, the conflict might bring together all the caste Hindus, including those which are just above the untouchability line, against the Scheduled Castes. Under the circumstances, the latter might look to conversion to another religion as a way out of their problems, and also, as a way of scoring off caste Hindus for their cursed hostility. But such a step might only worsen the situation, inviting even greater wrath from the Hindus of the entire region.

The benefits and concessions which the Scheduled Castes (and Tribes) are enjoying may be renewed for some more years. Their renewal is likely to figure as an issue in the near future. Political parties, anxious to secure the votes of the Scheduled Castes (and Tribes), will only be too eager to extend them for another decade. But in the process they may antagonize the other sections of the population, especially the castes just above the untouchability line who feel that they are lagging behind the Scheduled Castes in the gains they have made.

There is a positive aspect to the conflict between the dominant (and high) castes on the one hand, and the Scheduled Castes on the other, which is important, and needs to be mentioned. The bloodshed, death, rape and incendiarism have all to be viewed in the long run, as an integral part of the process of translating into reality the rights which the constitution of India grants to the Scheduled Castes and Tribes. To say this is not to condone the savage attacks on the Scheduled Castes, but only to recognize the important fact that the conflict has a positive dimension, it attracts a good deal of media attention. As a result, questions are asked in Parliament and the State legislatures, voluntary bodies visit the scene of conflict, and the police, who are generally reluctant to take action against the powerful village leaders, are forced to act. More importantly, there is a general raising of consciousness about the rights of the Scheduled Castes, and the latter become aware of the fact that they have supporters and friends in the world outside their village. If social conflict is indispensable to the improving of the living conditions of the Scheduled Castes, then its presence is a healthier sign than its absence.*

1. Before any measures and strategies could be adopted there is need to know the types and causes of poverty. This could be done by sponsoring village level survey by competent groups. Governments while arranging for such surveys should take care that information on all factors such as income, availability and access to social amenities, housing, dietary levels etc. location of the areas inhabited by the poor are taken into account;
2. Availability of infrastructural facilities, agricultural production levels, housing needs etc, are some of the factors that should also be considered to demarcate areas with large incidence of poverty. Governments especially of Afro Asian countries should locate such areas on the basis of above mentioned factors;
3. For quantifying poverty, it is essential to know the nature of poverty and also to have a comprehensive and updated data base. Necessary steps need therefore to be taken to strengthen the data base regarding all aspects of poverty viz. income, consumption expenditure, basket of goods in the normal diet;
4. Alleviation of poverty can be successful if the indirect causes such as literacy levels, bonded labour,

---

***Source**: Adopted from the Chapter "On Living in a Revolution" by Sri M.N. Srinivas, problems of International Co-operation, – "viertel jahres berichte" December 1987

exploitation by land owners etc, are also dealt with. Governments of the developing countries may like to take necessary steps in that direction;

5. The poverty line expressed in terms of consumption expenditure is by far the most common determinant of poverty. As the consumption expenditure for availing the basic necessities of food, clothing and shelter may vary depending on dietary habits, availability of natural resources and attitude to subsistence, the economic system of the country in question has to be studied in detail for quantifying poverty. Governments of the Afro-Asian Rural Reconstruction Organizations (AARRO) member countries may take necessary steps towards that direction.
6. Parity of income is a factor that should be kept in mind while determining poverty through the poverty line. The poverty line, which is expressed in terms of consumption expenditure, may vary from region to region depending on the parity of income of the population. A basket of goods may not cost the same in two countries and, therefore, it will be wrong to use the same expenditure levels for determining the poverty line. Although the World Bank specifies the range of $ 275-$370 per capita per annum, it is necessary that each country should determine its own poverty line depending on the cost of living prevalent in that country. This may also vary for different regions in the same country.
7. According to the World Development Report, poverty has been defined as "the inability to attain a minimum standard of living." The concept of a minimum standard of living" has two elements; one that can be measured in real terms like cost of basic necessities, and the other which is subjective including the cost of participating in every day life of society, such as education levels, entertainment facilities etc. An index, therefore, needs to be framed considering the factors such as health, education, and other social amenities

apart from consumption expenditure for determining the poverty line;

8. It has been observed that poverty is widespread in the rural areas of the developing countries which are largely dependent on agriculture. Agricultural production is thus closely related to the incidence of poverty in years of scarce rainfall, agricultural production is low and a majority of the population is deprived of their only source of income. Governments of the AARRO member countries should, therefore, ensure that alternative sources of income are made available to them and poverty alleviation programmes are taken up particularly in water deficient areas;
9. Countries which suffer from the problems of poverty have devised various measures for its alleviation. Some countries have been more successful in dealing with this problem than others. Programmes for alleviation of poverty in the AARRO member countries should therefore be studied and evaluated for their levels of success in a common forum. The successful strategies should be mutually studied and exchanged so that poverty could be fought on a global level. Once the effective strategies have been identified, they need to be suitably modified before the transfer of technology to other countries. Various factors affecting poverty, unique to a country need careful consideration while modifying these strategies. There is thus a need for a closer cooperation among AARRO member countries in this direction;
10. In many less developed countries poverty is not only a rural characteristic but also often times is parallel with agriculture (under-development and under-employment). Although improvements in labour and land productivities can be a source of income improvements through multiple cropping, planting of high value crops and undertaking of similar activities, etc. and therefore should be further promoted. The stimulus for integration and linkages with other sectors in particular manufacturing offer further

opportunities for marketing agricultural surplus and utilization of farm labour in higher value-added off-farm and/or non-agriculture employment. Agro-based industrialization in rural areas is very effective in generating additional employment and income in these areas. Agro-based industries should therefore be developed so as to use locally available raw materials, expertise and labour;

11. A majority of the rural poor under poverty consists of landless laborers. Their income is restricted to the seasonal demand of labour for on –farm activities. Agro-based industrialization is one way of providing them with alternative sources of income during the off- seasons. Cooperative is another way of organising the landless labourers for productive use. Allied sectors such as dairy, poultry, fisheries, handicrafts etc. need to be developed for providing income to the rural poor. Specific alleviation programmes should be devised keeping the landless labourers in mind. Besides providing them with alternative sources of income and their social condition has also to be improved through these programmes by making available education, health and recreation facilities to them;

12. Long-term poverty alleviation measures can be effective only if they take into account developments in the entire economy. Factors such as macro-economic policies, development of agriculture, infrastructure, rural industries, health, nutrition, sanitation, water supply, education etc. have all to be considered while formulating the long-term measures, close cooperation of all the agencies involved in these areas is imperative and necessary steps need to be taken for coordinating the attitude towards the achievement of these objectives;

13. Specific programmes of poverty alleviation should have specific objectives and approaches. Different regions suffering from poverty will need different programmes as the causes of poverty will vary depending on the socio-economic conditions of the people. The immediate

concern should be to provide the basic amenities for subsistence to the poor;

14. The Integrated Rural Development Programme (IRDP) is an important instrument of the strategy to alleviate poverty. The objective of such a programme, which has been successful in some member countries, is to assist the families below poverty line in rural areas by taking up self-employed agro-based ventures. The other developing countries should take up this programme modified according to their local conditions and provide income generating assets including working capital through a package of assistance comprising subsidy and institutional credit;
15. The broader area-based IRDP approach to rural development whilst useful in many cases has limitation in the sense that being a general and non-focused approach, leakages have taken place and the poor have not fully benefited from such projects. A specially and directly targeted approach bearing upon the identified poor could be more effective either independently and/or in combination with IRDP approach. Such an approach should not be precluded in the package of measures to tackle poverty;
16. Another programme which could usefully be taken up by the member countries of AARRO is Minimum Needs Programme. In India, this was designed to secure to the rural areas within a reasonable time frame, certain basic amenities in the field of education, health, drinking water, electrification, roads and home sites and it has been a great success;
17. The Malaysian experience shows that industrialization is the fastest means to alleviate rural poverty. Governments of the member countries may, therefore, consider the possibility of locating the industries/factories in rural areas which will alleviate rural poverty. To attract the industrialists to come to rural areas for setting up industries, suitable incentives may be provided. This will also serve the purpose of bringing down migration from rural to urban areas

and will reduce pollution problem in large cities/towns. In this context, it would be worthwhile to mention that most of the developing countries are shifting the already established factories from urban to rural areas at a very high cost to combat problems created by pollution;

18. Studies in Malaysia have brought out that the development and adoption of improved technology was instrumental for increased productivity, output and income to farmers. The availability of credit facilities and use of improved farm production technology have resulted in enhanced productivity and income. The Governments of the AARRO member countries are, therefore, well advised to make available to the farmers credit on easy terms, for at least for the increased net cost whenever a new improved technology is introduced this will facilitate taking up the new technology by the farmers;
19. Governments may provide adequate facilities for small scale and cottage industries to be set up in rural areas on cooperative basis. Credit facilities at concessional rates may also have to be provided at least in the beginning for the success of the project. Governments may also arrange for marketing of the products so that those engaged in small scale and cottage industries could get remunerative prices for their products;
20. For the efficient management of any rural development programmes initiated either by the Government or voluntary organization, people's participation is necessary. The Government should take necessary steps to decentralize the decision making process within the framework of national policy, promote local government institutions and increase the delegation of responsibility to other rural

· In view of its vital importance for success of any programme meant for the development of especially rural people a separate chapter is included on people's participation.

masses for rural development activities. The peoples' participation approach should also encompass self-help and self-initiated schemes and projects;

21. Cooperatives play a leading role to bring about effective social change and improvement in the rural economy which will result in alleviation of poverty. As such, the Government should encourage multi-purpose rural cooperative activities, such as, production, marketing, credit and human resource development. The cooperative members should be encouraged and motivated to take initiative in developmental activities thereby creating more avenues for rural employment.

22. The contribution of Non-Government Organizations (NGOs) is very effective in activities related to rural development programmes which are aimed at helping the rural poor. Governments should encourage, promote and support voluntary agencies as these grass-root organizations could play a significant role to supplement and complement the role of Government in the management of rural development programmes. A case in point is the credit programme ala' the Grameen Bank of Bangladesh and implemented by an NGO in Malaysia as "Project Amanah Ikhtiar." NGOs can also act as a liaison between masses in the rural areas and the Government in ensuring smooth flow of funds and optimal utilization of resources;

23. International organizations should contribute liberally in the form of financial aid and human resource for rural development work for alleviation of poverty. The assistance from international organizations is vital for the developing countries which are starved of resources and trained manpower;

24. The women organizations should be associated with poverty alleviation programmes from the very beginning;

25. Concurrent monitoring to assess the stages of implementation and its evaluation at periodic interval is necessary to critically analyse achievement and

results of projects, programmes and policies vis-à-vis intended objectives. The Government should create the facilities for monitoring and evaluation of anti-poverty schemes. This will help in the adjustments of strategies in response to performance gaps and other problems of implementation;

26. It is desirable to create and build up a data base as this information, if suitably utilized, will enrich the management capability for successful implementation of projects. The Government should take necessary steps in that direction considering the importance of data and information to the policy makers, scholars and researchers which will assist in the formulation of policies and preparation of projects for poverty alleviation;

27. A number of poverty alleviation programmes have been introduced by the various member countries at different points of time. These programmes vary with conditions in various countries and the causes of poverty. There is a need to train the staff responsible for the eradication of poverty, particularly when a new programme is introduced. There is also a need for training whenever an improved technology, successful in some of the countries is to be transferred to and adopted by developing countries. To train both trainers and farmers in particular. In alleviation programmer and projects including self-help projects and to exchange knowledge and expertise to other countries with experts from other countries, a need has been felt to have an institute having requisite facilities for training as well as for research.*

LESSONS LEARNED

Unless the poor take interest and recognize their own capability, external support may not help to bring about change in their condition. Even if inputs were externally

---

***Source**: Adopted from the Report of International Workshop on "Rural Poverty And Ways & Means to Alleviate It" Malecca, Malaysia, January, 1992.

injected without considering the value system and needs of the beneficiaries, programmes might not be sustainable once the external support is withdrawn. Thus a feeling of self-reliance has to be generated. Programme intervention should only follow when there is real will among the intended beneficiaries to change their condition. This requires attitudinal change on their part. Likewise the external agency should not unnecessarily raise their expectations. What was most important was to raise awareness and help the beneficiaries to develop a feeling of self-reliance. For that, awareness generating measures in the form of functional literacy programmes etc. could be initiated.

It was also desirable for any external agency to have a change agent on the spot. The change agent, first of all, should observe the value system of the intended beneficiaries and their ways of life, and make them aware of their potentials and limitations as a way of gaining their confidence. Once the confidence was gained and the change agent felt assured that the external input would not be detrimental to the feeling of self-reliance, he/she should try to obtain the support for the income-generating activities that the beneficiaries themselves had decided on. It was advisable to explore activities which were traditional and family-based and which had market value, and accordingly to assist beneficiaries to design the programmes for their benefit.

Poverty reduction was a time-consuming process, in which one faced ups and downs. Often times, it was a frustrating exercise. Hence, the programme period had to be reasonably long so that sufficient time could be devoted to establishing rapport with beneficiaries.

The beneficiaries of a programme have to take interest and recognize their own capabilities in order for external support to be effective. Sensitizing programme management of the needs and priorities in setting programme goals is essential to the success of a programme. It is therefore desirable for any external agency to have some body in the form of a change agent at the programme site that should observe the value system of the intended beneficiaries, their way of life, and make them aware of their potentials and limitations as a way of gaining their confidence. It is advisable to explore the activities which have been traditionally family based and have a market value, and assist the beneficiaries to design programmes based on these activities.

The question of poverty alleviation is a stupendous task. In the name of humanity the entire administrative system and all sections of people need recognize the deplorable conditions of living by the poor. Though, efforts have been there in the past, they were not strong and fully action oriented atleast now in the twenty first century in the name of humanity respecting the precious life of people suffering in the mire of poverty everyone should strive to work **Unto To The Last.***

***Source:** Adopted from the material *"Employment Strategies for The Rural Poor"*, United Nations, New York, 1994.

CHAPTER 15

Conclusion

The question of ameliorating the living conditions and the image of Dalits in India is a highly complex phenomenon. The State realising economic and social destitute conditions of living on the part of the Dalits in India have brought in some relevant constitutional and administrative measures towards uplifting them. Of several issues in India and the world over the most challenging and highly sensitive issue is in meeting social justice to the Dalits in India. Mere constitutional, legislative and administrative measures though relevant, appropriate and highly needed measures towards ameliorating largely deplorable conditions of living among the Dalits are essential.

The attitude on the part of the higher caste groups vis-à-vis the Dalits in India is deep rooted in the psyche or mindset of the so called higher caste groups. To improve the living conditions of the Dalits and to treat them as human beings as other ethnic groups are treated, is the kind of change that is to emerge amongst all sections of the so called higher caste groups.

Political leaders under some compulsion, social reformers with genuine objectives and social workers with real earnestness would advocate and work towards treating the Dalits as equals with regard and respect. It is natural expectation on the part of an individual, group, community or society to be treated with respect and acceptance. Here, not as a question of deviation, we may point out every individual and in the context of India every ethnic group feels proud of its ethnicity and expects that the ethnic group is recognised and respected. Unfortunately, with the emergence of *Varna* and ramification of caste hierarchy in India, it has become very difficult to apply the egalitarian principle of equality, recognition and dignity on the part of each ethnic group. As we have briefly discussed in the previous chapters in the book, the local institutions, the youth and the local leaders have a very challenging vital role to play for decades or centuries to fight and work towards social emancipation and better living conditions of the Dalits who constitute nearly 1/7th of India's population.

As a human being it is the moral responsibility on the part of every man and woman in India to understand, appreciate the injustice meted out to the Dalits over centuries and strive to undue the injustice meted out to them and work towards ameliorating their living conditions with a religious commitment. The fabric of caste system and the position of the Dalits in the system has become so rigid and deep rooted, it may take a long time to gradually dismantle the graded hierarchy of the caste system. Though the question of rectifying and remedying the social injustice meted out to the Dalits is quite apparent, that people in general cannot simply live with the knowledge of injustice, differential treatment meted out to the Dalits.

The one effective way towards improving the psyche, image and the living conditions of the Dalits is one may have to think of initiative and action on the part of the Dalits as well as on the part of the higher caste groups. Working together with the Dalits is not that easy. For centuries on, the Dalits have been socially distanced treating them as inferior to the higher caste Hindus. To work with a commitment and sense of understanding of equality among the Dalits and so called higher caste groups is an arduous task. Though we call it as something arduous task we cannot ignore it. Sincere and committed measures are essential to eradicate the lowly and inferior status of the Dalits in the Indian society. We are not simply talking of an upsurge or a revolution but we as people of this country feel ashamed of the way in which we looked upon and treated the Dalits as sub-human beings. It is not a question of regret and remorse on the part of the higher caste groups but to come down and realise and act towards recognising the Dalits as human beings.

It is said and it is true that human life is the highest kind of positive terminal in the evolutionary process. Human being is the only one who has developed and learnt verbal communication and the being who can think and reflect on multifarious aspects related to the life and the universe. Here we are not going into any philosophy or evolutionary advent of man on this planet. Man is gifted with (may be on learning) the sense of good and bad, right and wrong and justice and injustice. The other species, ancestors to mankind did not have this kind of faculty. It is said all human beings are born equal. For a moment when we reflect on human expectations on behaviour, normally and logically every human individual man or woman wants to be recognised, respected and treated as equally important fellow being.

No one would like to be treated as inferior whatever may be his age, sex and occupation and other accomplishments in life. It is a universal fact of human nature that every body wants to be respected and recognised. Not that they would like to be treated as princes and kings and great personalities but as simple humble human beings who are to be recognised and respected.

We are not simply emphasising on human individuality and dignity. We mention this in respect to the ways in which the Dalits all over India were treated for centuries as sub-human beings and menials. This horrible behaviour still continues in a little bit modified form.

One may write volumes and lecture for hours together that the Dalits are to be treated with due recognition and respect. Unfortunately, the views and ideas passed on by older generation (may be they thought it was right) were simply imbibed and carried over by successive generations in respect to the way in which that the Daltis are to be treated and interacted with. Today, in the 21st century as a result of constitutional measures, education, gradually growing public opinion, positive towards Dalits, enforcement of law, awareness among the Dalits themselves and fear of legal consequences in ill treating the Dalits, we find some growing change in the higher caste behaviour with some reluctance.

Because of the inherited burden of prejudice, the caste Hindus try to treat the Dalits and interact with them treating them as inferior to them. In majority of instances there was no question of any reflection and logic employed the way in which the Dalits were treated as menial and sub-human. We may call this as a pathetic, painful, tragedy in the life of the Dalits in India.

As we have mentioned earlier there is a need for democratic upsurge on the part of the Dalits and meaningful, relevant, justified change of attitude on the part of the higher caste-Hindus *vis-à-vis* the Dalits in India.

It is a massive problem not confined to one higher caste or a region but unfortunately spread over the entire sub-continent of India. Society and life are not static. It is dynamic. May be after few decades the posterity of India will see that the Dalits and other caste Hindus interact with each other as equals and there is no question of any superior or inferior ethnic community in India and all are one without any distinction whatsoever. Any sensible man would see, may be after a few centuries the question of untouchability and discriminatory treatment meted out to the Dalits was only a historical fact. It is not simply a wish, but the day will come that every body irrespective of caste and religion will be treated as respectable human beings.

Index

❑❑❑